TEARS OF A CLOWN

★ ★

TEARS OF A CLOWN

GLENN BECK AND THE
TEA BAGGING OF AMERICA

DANA MILBANK

DOUBLEDAY

NEW YORK LONDON TORONTO

SYDNEY AUCKLAND

DD

DOUBLEDAY

Copyright © 2010 by Dana Milbank

All rights reserved. Published in the United States by
Doubleday, a division of Random House, Inc., New York,
and in Canada by Random House of Canada Limited, Toronto.

www.doubleday.com

DOUBLEDAY and the DD colophon are registered trademarks
of Random House, Inc.

Cataloging-in-Publication Data is on file with the Library
of Congress

ISBN 978-0-385-53388-1

First Edition

In memory of Woodrow Wilson:

fascist, communist, president

CONTENTS

★ ★

CONTENTS

TEARS OF A CLOWN

★ ★

INTRODUCTION

* *

"Well, hello America!"

That greeting, at the start of most every Glenn Beck television broadcast, precedes the Fox News host's reading of the news of the day. To Beck, this news generally takes the form of a warning, such as this one broadcast during the health-care debate: "America is burning down to the ground, and if somebody doesn't ask these questions, well, we're all just going to watch it burn down together."

Having imparted this information to his viewers, Beck transitions to movement leader, proposing a way to help his viewers avoid the doomsday scenario he has just outlined. "Come on, America—let's go!" he says, waving the viewers, Fred Rogers–style, over to his set. "Follow me."

Those who have heeded the "follow me" cry have been taken by Beck to some unusual places: They've heard him talk about Barack Obama's "deep-seated hatred for white people," about the fact that he "can't debunk" the allegation that the U.S. government has set up concentration camps in Wyoming, about his wish to kill Michael Moore, and about his fantasy of poisoning Nancy Pelosi. They've followed along as he's described his mortal enemies, "progressives," as both communists and Nazis bent on one world government—planning a "Reichstag moment" for the United States and using "the same tactic" Hitler did in "rounding up Jews and exterminating them."

But tonight America, or some portion of it, has followed Beck to Norfolk, Virginia, where he's putting on a live performance in front of eight thousand paying customers along with fellow Fox News host Bill O'Reilly, who is a flamethrower in his own right but who next to Beck seems as mild as Jim Lehrer.

The SUVs parked in the garage next to the arena are plastered with magnetic yellow ribbons for the troops and decals of Christian fish symbols. They have bumper stickers promoting Sarah Palin and messages such as "Except for ending slavery, fascism, Nazism, and communism, war has never solved anything."

The audience members, some in camo, some with "Fight Socialism" T-shirts, and a few in the tricorn hats of the Tea Party, line up outside the arena, where local Tea Party activists pass out leaflets announcing future events. "Make your voice heard today before we lose our freedom to speak out," the Tea Party notice pleads. Tea Party candidates seeking the Republican nomination for the local congressional seat work the crowd.

Inside the arena, an exhaustive search of the thousands in the crowd finds three black people, other than those working the concession stands. The white faces mostly have gray hair, or none at all; the age of the audience is reflected in the kiosk inside the entrance promoting an assisted living facility and one of the sponsors of the event, a home health-care and hospice service. Surrounding the stage are some of the bodyguards in dark suits who follow Beck wherever he goes.

Beck begins his performance. In the second minute, he makes a mocking Hispanic accent while he talks about immigration. In the third minute, he advises the visiting Mexican president to "get your ass on your plane" and go home.

Just nine minutes after he has taken the stage, Beck is calling Obama "the Antichrist," using a deep, demonic voice to represent the president. "They're getting so tired of me saying there's a Marxist in the White House, I gotta take it up a notch," he explains.

Taking it up a notch seems always to be Beck's goal, and his recipe for success. Problem is, there aren't many notches left for him. After entertaining the crowd with a couple of penis jokes (about the name of Democratic congressman Anthony Weiner), he warns of an imminent takeover of the country by a global government: "Maybe it's better, then, that we just don't make it" as a civilization, "because they are building a global cage. They're building a machine to redistribute the wealth all over the globe."

O'Reilly joins Beck on the stage and teases his colleague about his apocalyptic forecasts. "I think we are so close to a perfect storm collapse, that if everything doesn't play out exactly right, you ain't going to make it," Beck informs O'Reilly. He agrees to a wager with O'Reilly, betting that within ten years, "the globe collapses."

The end is near! Beck's End Times prediction—grounded in a controversial prophecy of the Mormon faith he adopted a decade ago—is the sort of thing that has led Beck to replace O'Reilly as the most outrageous personality at Fox News. "He's worse than me!" O'Reilly tells the crowd, which applauds. When Beck arrived at Fox in 2009, "All of the heat went right over to you," he says to Beck. "It's great."

Great for O'Reilly, maybe—but what about the rest of us?

Beck declined to be interviewed for this book. He said on air before a single word had been written that it was a "smear." But as Beck himself said of Van Jones, one of the Obama administration officials he forced from office: "How is it that a smear campaign is conducted when you're only using the person's words? . . . Am I smearing him by using his own words?"

This book uses what Beck says is his own technique: quoting him in his own words. In Beck's case, these are some very special words.

At this writing, in the early summer of 2010, Beck has in the last few weeks: mocked the president's eleven-year-old daughter; praised Joseph McCarthy; recommended the work of an anti-Semitic author; released a "rooted in fact" thriller about the United States succumbing to a world government; marveled that a Sarah Palin biographer has not been punched in the face; and given his considered opinion that the private sector "could probably take care of things in Afghanistan better" than U.S. troops. Beck has been in what might be called an Ann Coulter spiral: Each outrage must pack more shock value than the previous. The difference is that Beck, unlike Coulter, has millions of passionate followers.

Around Memorial Day, Beck questioned the intelligence of Malia Obama, the president's eleven-year-old, after her father said at a press conference that she asked if he had yet been able to "plug the hole" leaking oil into the Gulf of Mexico.

"That's the level of their education, that they're coming to Daddy and saying, 'Daddy, did you plug the hole yet?' " Beck said in his radio show. With his sidekick imitating the president, Beck played young Malia in a radio skit and asked: "Why do you hate black people so much?"

"I'm part white, honey," said the sidekick, playing President Obama.

"Why, why, why, why do you still let the polar bears die?" Beck asked, in Malia's voice. "Daddy, why do you still let Sarah Palin destroy the environment? Why are—Daddy, why don't you just put her in some sort of a camp?"

Just days before his attack on the president's daughter, Beck had said on his radio show that the children of politicians should be off-limits: "We've never done anything but protect the families." Beck, recognizing the inconsistency, issued a rare apology. "I broke my own rule," he said. This rule had been broken many times before, as when he appeared on set with a walking cane to mock the limp of Obama's aunt. He called her "Tiny Tim" and pretended to beg for food like the Dickensian character.

There was no apology to the aunt. Then again, if Beck were to start apologizing to everybody he has offended, he'd have no time left for anything else. There was, for example, Beck's promotion on air of Nazi sympathizer Elizabeth Dilling's *The Red Network* from the 1930s. "McCarthy was absolutely right," he told radio listeners as he recommended Dilling's book in June. "He may have used bad tactics or whatever, but he was absolutely right." Dilling's book, he continued, was "doing what we're doing now"—documenting communists in America.

What Beck did not tell listeners is that Dilling referred to President Dwight Eisenhower as "Ike the kike" and President John Kennedy's New Frontier as the "Jew Frontier." Dilling made common cause with Adolf Hitler and blamed communism and the Second World War on the Jews. She considered interracial mixing to be a communist plot.

Strangely, at the same time Beck was peddling the work of this anti-Semite on the radio, he was attempting to convince his viewers on Fox News that the rest of the American media was part of an anti-Israel plot.

Beck, defending the Israeli government's deadly raid on a flotilla of peace activists, showed a video of Israeli commandos being beaten by the activists. "Turn on any media outlet—other than this one—they're not going to show you this," Beck told his viewers.

Had his viewers in fact turned on other media outlets, they would have discovered that the exact same footage had already aired, on CBS, NBC, ABC, CNN, MSNBC, PBS, Headline News, CNBC, and even, to the delight of Comedy Central's Jon Stewart, Univision. No matter: Beck's monologue with the false allegation wound up embedded in the Israeli foreign ministry's Web site.

It takes a certain intellectual gift to be able to recommend an anti-Semitic tract at the same time you are using a phony allegation to accuse others of being anti-Israel. Beck can do this because he is not constrained by the fact/fiction divide that governs the rest of the news business. Beck calls his unique hybrid of fact and fiction "faction."

"Faction," Beck explained, is a "completely fictional"

account that somehow still has a plot "rooted in fact." That is what Beck wrote in the foreword to his thriller, *The Overton Window*, which came out in mid-June. After providing a "fictional" account of world government taking over America, he offered a thirty-page afterword full of citations of "factual" events that supposedly support the fictional story.

"What makes this thing a thriller and terrifying is the fact that it is, a lot of it, happening," Beck explained on the radio. "Now it is a fictional story, but it really—who knows who the players are, but the words that the villain uses are right out of progressive speeches. The things that happen could happen in America."

And what is this that "could happen in America"? From Beck's book, pages 210 to 211: "What we've finally come to understand, Noah, is that the people can't be trusted to control themselves. Even the brightest of them are still barbarians at heart . . . The American experiment has failed, and now it's time for the next one to begin. One world, one government—not of the people this time, but the right people: the competent, the wise and the strong."

Faction is a dangerous thing—presenting readers, viewers, and listeners with a fictitious account and making them think that it is true. But for millions of Beck radio listeners, Fox viewers, and book buyers, it is a compelling form.

His average of 2.8 million nightly viewers for his Fox

show in early 2010 put him second only to O'Reilly in all of cable news; if Beck had a prime-time slot like O'Reilly, he would almost certainly be number one. His weekly average of nine million radio listeners puts him behind only Rush Limbaugh and Sean Hannity. His books have sold more than three million copies—and other books he touts on air become overnight bestsellers. *Forbes* magazine put his revenues at an annual $32 million.

In the 2010 Time 100, Beck's entry was written by a starstruck Palin—perhaps the only figure in America who equals Beck in stature among the Tea Party crowd. "Who'd have thought a history buff with a quirky sense of humor and a chalkboard could make for such riveting television?" she gushed. "Though he sometimes dismisses himself as an aw-shucks guy or just a 'rodeo clown,' he's really an inspiring patriot who was once at the bottom but now makes a much needed difference from the very, very top."

His typical viewers, judging from his advertisers, are old, conservative, and in financial and medical distress. In addition to the ads for patriotic and family-values groups, there are solicitations for the indebted (Credit Answers, IRSTaxAgreements.com, Mortgage Relief Hotline), for the ailing (Arriva Medical diabetic supplies, the Scooter Store, PremierCare walk-in tubs), and for those who fear economic collapse (gold dealers Goldline, Lear Capital, Rosland Capital).

Some Beck critics think Beck has gone about as far as he can with the distressed-and-angry demographic. The liberal group Media Matters has seen a "summer swoon" in Beck's TV audience, to under two million for some shows from a peak of over three million earlier in the year.

But forecasts of a more lasting swoon may be too hopeful. Beck has transcended the role of entertainer and talk-show host and now finds himself at the front of an antigovernment movement. The de facto leader of the Tea Party activists, he has fueled tax-day protests across the land and organized mass protests in Washington on September 12, 2009, and August 28, 2010.

At the end of 2009, Gallup asked Americans which living man anywhere in the world they admire most. More volunteered Beck than offered the pope, Bill Gates, Billy Graham, Bill Clinton, or George H. W. Bush. The only man to be mentioned more often than Beck was South Africa's Nelson Mandela.

These Beck admirers do more than worship the man; they obey his every pronouncement. Beck, in an interview with the *New York Times* in early 2009, said, "I say on the air all the time, 'if you take what I say as gospel, you're an idiot.'" In fact, Beck often does the opposite, demanding "Where am I wrong?" and pointing out that the red phone, supposedly a hotline for which only the White House has the number, never rings to correct him.

And there are, evidently, a lot of what Beck would describe as "idiots" accepting his broadcasts as gospel. A Harris poll in March 2010 found that a majority of Republicans consider Obama to be a "socialist" who "has done many things that are unconstitutional" and "wants to turn over the sovereignty of the United States to a one-world government"—the very themes that Beck has championed above all others.

When Utah Republicans in May 2010 kicked out longtime Republican senator Robert Bennett (who took the conservative position 84 percent of the time over his career) in favor of a Tea Party candidate to serve as their nominee, Beck gave his viewers credit for "what happened to Bob Bennett in Utah." He issued a warning: "People in Washington, you should be terrified."

The very same day Utah conservatives were purging themselves of Bennett, the Republican Party of Maine abandoned its old platform—a typical New England mix of free-market economics and conservation—and adopted a manifesto demanding abolition of the Federal Reserve, labeling global warming a "myth," insisting that the border be sealed, and, as a final plank, calling for a fight against "efforts to create a one-world government."

One world government? That idea could only have come from one place in the mass media. And, indeed, Beck was back on the air days later with more warnings about how "they"—Obama and friends—"are creating a global governance structure."

"Social and ecological justice and all of this bullcrap," Beck told his viewers, "is man's work for a global government." Beck tossed out phrases such as "global standards" and "global bank tax"—all part of a conspiracy by the "global government people." He further provided the revelation that "Jesus doesn't want a cap-and-trade system."

Beck has, in his nightly Fox broadcasts, all but abandoned the day's headlines in favor of historical rewrites and conspiracies mapped out on his chalkboard. When breaking news intervenes, Fox is forced to preempt Beck's lectures and bring in a Fox newsreader—often prompting howls of protest from Beck loyalists.

Beck has essentially created a parallel universe for his viewers. On the day Obama nominated Elena Kagan to the Supreme Court, Beck omitted that news in favor of a fanciful report about the administration's attempt to drive conservatives off the airwaves. On the day *USA Today* had the headline "Tax Bills in 2009 at Lowest Level Since 1950," Beck skipped that, instead saying he doesn't want the government getting involved in the Internet "at least until people aren't worshiping Satan, you know, in office." (Beck maintained later that he really wasn't, contrary to appearances, "saying that Obama was a Satan worshiper.")

The Anti-Defamation League identified the secret to Beck's success when it noted that he, unlike other prominent right-wing talkers, was willing "to give a platform to the conspiracy theorists and anti-government extremists." But he does it in the most disarming way—with props, costumes, gags, imitations, and on-air crying jags. Watching the shtick of the forty-six-year-old recovering alcoholic and cocaine addict, typical Beck viewers probably have no idea he is introducing them to some of the most controversial fields of Mormon theology, such as the White Horse Prophecy, which envisions the Latter-day Saints rescuing the U.S. Constitution.

Ultimately, only Beck knows if he actually believes the things he says on air. Given his background as a pro-choice, ponytail-wearing, drug-using DJ on morning radio, it's tempting to think he invented the conservative persona, and found the ideology, to exploit a market opportunity. Anger and fear always grow in times of economic trouble—and Beck's arrival at Fox News in early 2009 just after the American economy collapsed could not have been better timed. Yet even if Beck embraced the ideology for entirely commercial reasons, it's entirely possible that, after playing the role for so long on radio and TV, he has internalized it.

Whatever is going on inside the head of Beck, he is, on the outside, a singular performer. "Enjoy the performance," says the ticket taker at the Constant Convocation Center at Norfolk's Old Dominion University before Beck and O'Reilly take the stage for their "Bold & Fresh Tour."

Giant screens inside advertise a coming appearance by

Michael Bublé in his "Crazy Love Tour"—but tonight the crazy love is mostly for Beck. Beck takes the stage in blue jeans, sneakers, and a loosened tie adorning his dress shirt. He shifts seamlessly from phallic jokes to End Times theology. "I've been talking about a perfect storm coming for five years," he says. "I've been talking about exactly what's happening now, coming for five years."

He marvels that his followers are not more violent. "Think how we've been pushed to the wall. You've been called a racist, you've been called a hater, you've been called a terrorist—and yet, God bless America, nobody has done anything stupid."

Phrases of paranoia and desperation tumble forth: "I don't want to live like this . . . Republic's at stake! . . . They're telling you lies . . . Don't you want to live in the country that we thought we lived in?" Beck starts to cry. He gives a version of Martin Luther King Jr.'s "I've Been to the Mountaintop" speech. "I have been a lonely voice for a very long time, and no longer!" he says. "You can do whatever the hell you want with me. You will replace me."

O'Reilly has his own routine, including a fake Chinese accent and a brief acting-out of the late Ted Kennedy at Chappaquiddick. But in comparison with Beck, he is downright sunny. "I obviously have a different take on the world than Beck does," O'Reilly says. Beck "just runs all the way down the field," while O'Reilly goes "step by step."

But here in Norfolk, Beck's view has prevailed. Beck polls the audience about whether they believe, as he does, that the modern world will collapse within a decade. Most in the hall applaud. He asks whether they agree with O'Reilly that a ten-year forecast for the world's demise is "unreasonable." There is relative silence.

Beck shoots an apologetic glance at O'Reilly. "Look," he says. "I don't want to be right. I don't."

"You're not going to be right," O'Reilly fires back sharply.

But O'Reilly misses the point. People don't follow Glenn Beck because he is right. They follow him out of fright.

CHAPTER 1

CRYING ALL THE WAY TO THE BANK

. . . .

"I think I'm gonna need more tears," Glenn Beck is saying.

The makeup woman is skeptical, but she comes over to rub some more menthol ointment under his eyes. "A teeny bit," she allows.

The Fox News host fans himself to get the vapors closer to his eyes. He holds his eyelids open. "I think my eyes are getting used to it," he laments.

Finally, the tears come. He puckers his lips. His eyes are glistening. Glenn Beck is crying again.

"Just look at me," the photographer instructs him. Beck looks miserable. The photographer is satisfied. "Instant sadness," she says.

Beck has built his career on tears. On his Fox News show, he cries about his family. He cries about other people's families. He cries because he loves his country. He cries because of death panels. He cries because Barack Obama is turning the country into Nazi Germany, or possibly the Soviet Union or Communist China, or maybe just France.

On this sea of tears, Beck's boat has floated to the top of cable news and talk radio, and put him at the head of a mass antigovernment conservative movement. The tears have made Beck rich and famous—and now, for the photo shoot, he's having himself a good, chemically induced cry.

"Try to keep your eyes open," the photographer counsels as Beck battles the menthol fumes. "I know it's probably, like, impossible."

Beck pouts. The tears flow freely. "You've even got a new runny nose," the photographer observes. The host informs her that those are in fact tears dripping from his nose.

"Wow," Beck says as the ointment kicks in. His lower lip is curled down, his chin puckered.

"What if you were laughing and crying at the same time?" the photographer proposes. "Yeah, yeah. Open your mouth, I think, is good."

Beck is now crying like a baby, red-faced and sobbing. Those in the room laugh as he attempts a silent scream.

"Open your mouth really big, like you're wailing. Eyes big, too—make your eyes big."

Beck obliges, and sticks out his tongue for added effect.

"Try to sit up straight," the photographer asks. "Sorry, too much instruction," she apologizes. Now: "Look up to the heavens. Like, curse—curse God."

Beck pretends to curse God. The photographer laughs.

"Put your face a little more toward me. That's good. Eyes bigger if you can. Can you open them any more? Look like you're horrified."

"Horrified?" Beck asks. He adopts a horrified look. It's a wide-eyed, shocked look.

"That's good. Your eyes are really watering." Beck now looks stunned. "What if you're laughing?" she asks.

"Ha! Ha! Ha!" The weeping Beck laughs. He raises his hands, like a mad scientist.

"No hands, actually," the photographer says.

★ ★ ★

Glenn Beck cried on his very first day on the job. Call it opening-day jitters.

After a successful run at CNN, Beck had just switched to a more logical home, Fox News, where he was about to turn the sleepy 5 P.M. time slot into a cultural phenomenon. His first show was January 19, 2009, on the eve of President Obama's inauguration. His guest: Sarah Palin, the failed 2008 Republican vice presidential candidate.

"I first started reading about her last spring, when she gave birth to her son Trig," Beck began. He got no further. His voice started to catch. "I'm the dad of a special needs child," he said, choking up at the mention of his grown daughter with cerebral palsy. "And we had something in common." He soldiers on, bravely and with great difficulty. "And I called her up because I just was moved by the way she reacted to the birth of her child. She was real. I for once didn't feel so alone." Beck still had not fully composed himself. "This is before the media circus, before all the political bullcrap," he continued. "Sarah Palin was just a mom of five doing a job that needed to be done. She was my kind of leader."

The image of the Alaska governor appeared on the screen. Beck was no longer crying. "You are one hot grandma," he said. "I'm just sayin'."

★ ★ ★

Once he hit the Fox airwaves, Beck's rise was meteoric. Unfortunately, he had no time to enjoy it. This is because the end of the world was coming. And this made Glenn Beck cry.

"Every time you turn that television on," he said in his March 13, 2009, broadcast, "it just seems like the whole world is spinning out of control." Particularly if your television is tuned to Fox News at 5 P.M. Eastern Time.

"War. Islamic extremism. Europe on the brink. Even pirates now," Beck went on. ". . . Six thousand were killed or beheaded on our border just last year . . . Our companies faced new union mandates and global cap-and-trade and the second-highest corporate tax rate in the world . . . Meanwhile, over four million friends and neighbors have lost their jobs in the last four months alone . . . What happened to the country that loved the underdog and stood up [for] the little guy? What happened to the voice of the forgotten man? The forgotten man is you."

He then recalled a better time. A time when George W. Bush was president. A time when we had just been attacked by terrorists. "Our hearts were full of terror and fear," Beck narrated. "We came together . . . On September 12th, and for a short time after that, we really promised ourselves that we would focus on the things that were important— our family, our friends, the eternal principles that allowed America to become the world's beacon of freedom."

The camera was on Beck, who was still backstage. He hadn't even walked onto his set yet, and he was already *ferklempt*.

"Are you ready to be that person that you were that day?" he asked, stifling a sob. "After 9/11, on 9/12. I told you for weeks, you're not alone." Beck could not hold back the tears. He looked at the ceiling to try to regain control of himself. "I'm turning into a freaking televangelist," he said in exasperation.

You think?

But Beck was becoming more than a televangelist. He was installing himself as leader of a new movement, the 9/12 Project, which would have a mass march on Washington on, naturally enough, 9/12.

He showed images of people around the country who

would be his followers in this movement, going from a shot of Chuck Norris in Texas "to military bases in Iraq where real heroes have gathered." At the mention of the heroes, Beck choked up anew, cleared his throat, and soldiered on.

He was finally composed enough to walk out onto the set, this time decorated with a "We the People" backdrop. "The real power to change America's course still resides with you," he went on. "You are the secret, you're the answer." He started to cry again and put his hand on his chest. He looked down in an unsuccessful attempt to hold back the floodgates. "I'm sorry," he said. "I just love my country and I fear for it." He looked around, trying in vain to stop the tears. He wiped his eyes. "And it seems like the voices of our leaders and special interests and the media, they're surrounding us. And it's, it sounds intimidating, but you know what? Pull away the curtain. You'll realize that there ain't anybody there." He wiped away another tear—and, with that damp beginning, a movement was born.

★ ★ ★

Beck's tear ducts were fast becoming a very valuable organ. "Only in America," observed Senator Lindsey Graham of South Carolina, "can you make that much money crying."

Obviously a sensitive man, Beck addressed his lachrymose ways one night on TV. "Yes, I do, on this program, cry like a little girl sometimes. I'm sorry, actually, if that destroys my credibility with you." Actually, the credibility problem is what comes from his mouth, not his eyes, but that wasn't the point. "I've stopped hiding who I am and being ashamed of who I am a long, long time ago. And if you don't like it, that's okay. There are other shows on TV. Watch them. I am who I am, like it or not. Big girls don't cry, oh, but I do from time to time. Why? Because as I told you before, I feel passionately about my country, and the people in it."

Aww.

One of the exciting things about Beck's tears is you never know exactly when they will come. They caught viewers quite off guard on February 3, 2009, when he introduced an interview with William Slemaker, whose stepdaughter, Yvette Martinez, has been missing since 2004. "She disappeared just a few blocks away from our U.S. border," Beck said, then paused. He closed his mouth as the tears began to come. "Two years ago, I made her father a promise that I would not let this story dry—uh, die," he continued, eyes moist. "However, I had to break that promise," he said, pausing again to fight for his composure, "because I am now working"—another pause for composure—"at a network that will follow through on a story. I am not a journalist"—he is losing the battle with his emotions—"I'm just a guy who cares." He chokes up anew. "I'm sorry. I'm just a guy who cares an awful lot about my country. And I think you do, too. But sometimes, for political reasons or whatever reasons, people just won't follow a story."

He got through his interview with the stepfather relatively dry-eyed, then concluded: "It is a real blessing for me to be able to tell you, sir, that the cavalry has arrived. Fox is here, and we are doing everything we can, and we'll have you back, sir, and God bless."

"Glenn, thank you and everybody at Fox and I appreciate it and I hope to be back soon," Slemaker said.

That was the last time Slemaker or his stepdaughter was mentioned on Fox News, according to a search of transcripts. As for Beck's previous network, CNN reported on the Martinez case several times. So did the *New York Times*, ABC News, *People*, and *Time* magazine—all before it came to Beck's attention.

* * *

Beck was known to have himself a televised cry even before Fox came calling. In a 2008 interview, he wept while describing his recovery from the days when he was a "hopeless alcoholic, using drugs every day" and jobless. His future wife wouldn't marry him unless they had a mutual religion, and his friend suggested the Mormon Church. When he found out his daughter liked the church, "it was then I thought I don't care if there's Kool-Aid down in the basement. I'm drinking it because I want to be like that."

The tears were beginning to well. "We were baptized

on a"—Beck, choking up, cleared his throat—"baptized on a Sunday, and on Monday an agent called me out of the blue." The agent wanted to get Beck in touch with an executive at Clear Channel, the conservative radio outfit. "As he said that, no kidding"—Beck looked away and cleared his throat to fight back the tears—"my call waiting went off," and it was the man from Clear Channel himself. "I went back to my agent and he said, 'Wow, do you ever feel like someone upstairs is watching over you?' And I said"—here Beck choked up anew, then looked away—" 'Yes, sir, I do.' " He wiped away a tear.

★ ★ ★

These days, Beck has causes greater than himself to cry about—such as Obama's plan to impose Nazi population control methods on America. That's what he alleged on August 11, 2009, during the summer of the town-hall meetings aimed at sinking health-care reform.

"Tonight," he began, "we have a special on the czars"—that's what he calls many White House officials—"and some of the statements that should horrify America . . . particularly if you're elderly, handicapped, or have a very, very young child." In conspiratorial tones, Beck said he was "under a great amount of pressure to not bring you this news."

Beck maintained that he was "following the directions of the president of the United States," who had recommended people judge him by the advisers he selected. This, naturally, took Beck to Nazi eugenics, which he said originated with American "progressives" such as Woodrow Wilson and Teddy Roosevelt, the latter endorsing a book "that Hitler once referred to as his bible." Beck credited these American presidents for inspiring "the Nazi eugenic idea [which] evolved naturally into the eventual Holocaust and the deaths of six million Jews."

Still with him? "The builder of the master race was only part of the problem in Germany, made possible after they began to devalue life. They tried to figure out how much is a life worth, and put a price on how much each individual was worth—and some were worth more than others."

Here Beck began to feel the familiar sensation. He paused and looked down to stop the tears. "I want to show you a poster," he said, displaying a Nazi propaganda image making the case for weeding out the infirm, "and I want you to know that I have a daughter that was born"—his voice started to break—"with cerebral palsy"—more choking up—"and they said when she was born that she would never walk or talk"—pause for composure—"or feed herself." He cleared his throat, then, fighting tears, explained how the Nazi propaganda poster showing a man whose hand was severely disfigured "reminds me of my daughter's hand."

Recovering, Beck went on to compare the Nazis to the Obama administration, based on "what the president of the United States has told us today." He said the administration has "just started to print money" the way they did in Weimar Germany. "Is it possible that our debt is so high that we can't pay it back or we have to make tough decisions and possibly ration health care?" Beck asked. "The answer everyone will tell you is yes."

Beck explained, without benefit of actual fact, that Obama's advisers favor health-care rationing and even sterilants in the drinking water. He then endorsed Palin's allegation that Americans "will have to stand in front of Obama's death panel so bureaucrats can decide . . . whether they are worthy of health care."

Voilà! Beck had traced a line from Adolf Hitler's eugenics to Barack Obama's health-care plan, via Teddy Roosevelt and Woodrow Wilson. It's enough to make you want to cry.

★ ★ ★

Sometimes, the simplest thing can make Beck weep—even a cold soft drink. Once, during a discussion about why so many Obama advisers worship Chairman Mao, he took an unexpected turn and played the old TV commercial in which a boy offers his Coke to a roughed-up football player. "It's okay, you can have it," the boy says. Next, Beck played the old Kodak commercial with Paul Anka singing "Times of Your Life."

"If a politician told you right now that he could make that happen again, you could go back to those simpler times when people were together, you'd do it in a heartbeat, wouldn't you?" Beck asked. Then, the telltale pause. The crying was coming. "But the truth is"—Beck shook his head, looked down, and contorted his face to hold back the tears—"no politician could take you there.

"You know," he went on, still struggling for his voice, "America, we've been at a party that we weren't supposed to be at." He likened the nation to a kid going home past curfew and knowing "you're going to get your butt kicked." The thought of this, too, choked up Beck. He spoke about America forced "to stay home on a Saturday night because we're financially grounded." This proved so overwhelming that Beck struggled for nearly eleven seconds before completing his next thought.

"America, I apologize," he said. "I'm an emotional guy."

But not always when you expect him to be. On March 22, 2010, the day after health-care reform finally cleared Congress, Beck surprised his viewers. "I saw all kinds of Tweets today: 'Oh, Glenn Beck's goin' to cry.' No, I left that for the Kennedy clan. I'm not crying. Today I'm actually feeling thankful . . . I'm thankful that the Progressive Party has stepped out of the shadow and showed Americans who they really are."

A dry-eyed Beck? Must have run out of menthol.

CHAPTER 2

GOD SMILES ON A "RECOVERING DIRTBAG"

* *

The mayor of Glenn Beck's hometown of Mount Vernon, Washington, decided that the hamlet would have a "Glenn Beck Day" to honor its most famous son. And a Glenn Beck Day is exactly what the town got: thousands of riled up, angry people shouting at each other, and fears of violence.

Mayor Bud Norris invited Beck to receive the key to the city on September 26, 2009, the same day he was giving a speech in nearby Seattle. Beck accepted, and, according to local reports, brought with him a whole lot of trouble:

A petition signed by sixteen thousand people was delivered to officials in the town of thirty-one thousand demanding they call off the event. City officials were swamped with three thousand e-mails and several phone calls, including a couple of threatening messages.

A plane flew overhead with a banner proposing an

answer to giving Beck the key to the city: "Change the Locks." Lining the streets were eight hundred pro- and anti-Beck demonstrators—the largest disturbance Mount Vernon had ever seen—carrying signs and a giant effigy of the Fox News host portraying him as the tea (party) brewing "Mad Hater." At least one demonstrator was arrested.

Six of the seven members of the city council declined Norris's offer of tickets to the event, and the council passed a resolution declaring that it was "in no way sponsoring the mayor's event."

The city got a bill for the event for $17,748.85—mostly for a security detail that included men in black on roofs with binoculars—that blew a hole in the town's budget. The townsfolk who paid $25 a ticket to see Beck didn't come close to covering the cost.

A few years earlier, Beck had mocked his hometown in a book titled *The Real America*. "Mount Vernon, Washington, couldn't have been farther from where I wanted to be," he wrote. "It's a little community in Skagit Valley that, by the way, is the largest tulip producer outside of Holland. Whoopee!"

But on Glenn Beck Day, he ordered up some tears as he recalled going to the theater in town with his mother. "Now, I would give my right arm to live in a town like Mount Vernon," said Beck, who had grown from a lanky teen to a soft and pudgy six-foot-three. "And I discovered today that there are a ton of people ready to cut it off. It doesn't bother me, because I have the key to their house now."

As Beck was about to receive the key, the sound system malfunctioned in the hall. "It's a left-wing conspiracy!" one woman shouted, according to an account in the *Seattle Times*.

Beck, eschewing politics, recalled his Mount Vernon antics, which included the theft of chewing gum. He spoke fondly about the "magical place" of his youth, part of a "Norman Rockwell's America" that he still believes could prevail—if only people would stop "tearing each other apart."

Beck's idealized portrait of his hometown—and his wish that people would stop the sort of tearing apart that is his own trademark—captured a central Beckian contradiction. His personal narrative—overcoming his mother's suicide and years of drug and alcohol addiction to find God and love—is compelling and uplifting. Yet the message he broadcasts to millions is angry and apocalyptic.

Beck, born in 1964, had the makings of a happy childhood in Mount Vernon. His parents ran the bakery in town, which operated under the names Sweet Tooth Pastry and City Bakery. Of his early childhood, he told the *Deseret News* of Salt Lake City: "I'm a schmo. My family never made more than $25,000 a year. We're all bakers for generations." His parents sometimes dressed him and his sister up in Colonial garb to give the town a patriotic feel that might appeal to tourists. Young Beck, who attended a Catholic primary school, would also dress up in a tux and perform magic tricks.

"When I was eight years old my mom gave me an album called 'The Golden Years of Radio,'" he wrote. "I became mesmerized." He wanted to be a broadcaster, and got his first gig at the tender age of thirteen after winning a local station's contest to host an hour on air. While in high school, he was working as a professional DJ at Mount Vernon's KBRC, drinking Coca-Cola on the set. By eighteen, he had a highly successful morning show in the area.

But Beck's childhood was also full of pain and tragedy. His parents gave up on the bakery when downtown was decimated by the malls. His mother was an alcoholic and a drug addict, by Beck's account, and he lived with her after his parents divorced in 1977.

"My mother committed suicide when I was thirteen years old," Beck frequently says. He describes this as the source of both his pain and his strength: "My mom was a drug addict who committed suicide when I was thirteen. While that was a horrible and tragic event in my life, one that took me years to get beyond, in many ways it has ended up helping me become the person I am today. I am stronger because of it. I am wiser because of it."

This isn't exactly true. He was fifteen years old when

Mary Beck drowned in 1979. And the authorities at the time were not convinced it was a suicide rather than a mere accident. After the online publication *Salon* recently raised questions about the incident, the *News Tribune* of Tacoma, Washington, looked into it further.

Forty-one-year-old Mary Beck's body was found in Puget Sound, as well as that of a man who had taken her fishing on his small boat. An empty pint of Gordon's vodka was found on the abandoned boat. The Tacoma police report said Mary Beck "appeared to be a classic drowning victim," although the Coast Guard speculated that she could have jumped overboard, which would mean the other victim drowned trying to save her. In 2000, when he was working in Tampa, the *St. Petersburg Times* published a profile of Beck that reported that he "never told his first wife that his mother killed herself when he was a teenager. She found out when Beck told his radio listeners." In any event, fifteen-year-old Beck was brought to the Pierce County morgue, where a family friend identified his mother's body. Beck and an older sister then went to live with his father.

In truth, the details don't really matter. It's not a whole lot better to lose your mother to an accident when you are fifteen than to suicide when you are thirteen. In a novel loosely based on his childhood, *The Christmas Sweater*, Beck has the protagonist's mother die in a car accident when she falls asleep at the wheel. In a note accompanying that 2008 novel, Beck wrote that his mother "died when I was thirteen."

Still, the suicide became a key part of Beck's narrative. He told the *Deseret News* that a brother—a stepbrother by most accounts—later committed suicide, too, and another died young from a heart attack. Beck wrote in 2003 that he had contemplated taking his own life when he was working in Kentucky in his twenties. "There was a bridge abutment in Louisville, Kentucky, that had my name on it," he wrote. "Every day I prayed for the strength to be able to drive my car at seventy mph into that bridge abutment . . . I have those stories to tell my kids and say, 'Look, insanity runs in the family like a pack of wild elephants. Don't turn out like Grandma. Don't turn out like me.' "

Beck talks easily on air about his troubled family—"I have two suicides in my family" and "I come from a dysfunctional family"—but he has relatively little to say about his father, William Beck, who is still living. "My dad and I weren't very close to each other when I was growing up, because he was working all the time," Beck writes. "He and I were never close until later in life, when I sobered up," he writes elsewhere, saying his father has since become "the best friend I've ever had."

By contrast, his late maternal grandfather, Edward Lee Janssen, is a regular fixture in Beck's monologues, a symbol of hard work and frugality. He mentions how his grand-father got his family through the Depression, how he'd watch *The Lawrence Welk Show* with his grandparents on Saturday nights, and how his grandfather used the same handmade tool box for fifty years. "He never wanted a new one," Beck recalls with approval.

Railing against some form of government handout, Beck says people like his grandparents "would punch us in the face for needing something like this." They would have him "in the snow barefoot for a month cutting wood." He says his late grandparents, though Democrats, would join him in his dislike for modern Democrats. "The Democratic Party . . . left my grandparents, left my parents," he reports. "It is anti–everything my grandparents believed, and they were Democrats."

Beck also remembers his grandfather, a Boeing machin-ist and an auctioneer who didn't go past the fourth grade, as a great storyteller, a trait even Beck's detractors would say he has inherited. Edward Lee Janssen taught young Beck that there are three types of characters in good stories: "There's heroes, there's villains, and then there is the char-acter that is there but for the grace of God go I." Beck has employed each of these archetypes to great effect. It took him "a long time before I realized my grandfather was just making these stories up." Beck has apparently acquired this skill, too. He restored the chair his grandfather used when he told the stories and brought it on the Fox set to show his viewers.

By Beck's own account, he spent the fourteen-year period between 1980 and 1994 drunk and high. "I was taking drugs every day of my life since I was sixteen years old," he boasted to the *Deseret News*. At one point he was drinking a gallon of Jack Daniel's each week. By the age of twenty-four, he said, "I was making about $300,000 a year"—he had skipped college and gone straight into broadcasting—"and most of it went directly up my nose."

"If I hadn't been such a cheapskate, cocaine would have killed me," Beck writes. "I remember looking into the mirror one day and seeing crusted blood all over my face, from all the cocaine I had snorted the day before . . . I found other recreational drugs, like alcohol, to get into that were much more cost-effective and didn't make my nose bleed."

By the time he quit abusing substances in 1994, Beck reports, "The doctor gave me six months to live."

The addictions were destroying his career. Now he often mentions the young producer he fired for giving him a ballpoint pen rather than a Sharpie for autograph signing. "I don't even remember his name," Beck recalled for one audience, tearfully, his chin quivering.

The writer Alexander Zaitchik, in *Salon*, uncovered various similar anecdotes that Beck has been less eager to share in public. There was the time in Phoenix when Beck, on the air, called the wife of a rival a couple of days after she had a miscarriage—and joked about how his rival couldn't have a baby. In Kentucky, he routinely made fun of an obese woman who hosted a show on another station, using Godzilla sound effects and claiming that at her wedding "instead of throwing rice after the ceremony, they are going to throw hot, buttered popcorn."

In New Haven, Connecticut, Beck's last stop before he sobered up, he insulted on air yet another broadcaster at a sister station. The man, a retired hockey player, was so infuriated that he struck Beck in the head in the parking lot, the *Hartford Advocate* reported. The paper quoted a colleague as saying the man who assaulted Beck was "hailed as a hero" at both stations.

That's consistent with Beck's own description of himself from the time: "I was a monster," "I was a scumbag," "I'm a recovering dirtbag."

Beck's on-air performance deteriorated as the drugs and alcohol took hold, causing him to bounce around from town to town—Houston, Baltimore, Washington, Corpus Christi, Provo, Louisville, Phoenix—finally winding up at KC101 in New Haven. "There's nothing like being eighteen years old in the fifth largest market in America, and then spending the next dozen years dropping ninety-seven spots," Beck writes.

The depressing confines of KC101 were located on a

suburban road in Hamden, Connecticut. The site includes a corrugated metal building sitting behind a drab red-brick building in a weedy field across from an elementary school. The radio towers spring from the weeds. Here, the addicted Beck found himself doing such dignified things as dressing in a plush banana costume for a radio promo.

It was around then that Beck, living in a nineteenth-century farmhouse in the next town, Cheshire, divorced his first wife. He says he blacked out while telling his girls a bedtime story and couldn't remember it the next morning. He spent time with his "good friend and physician for many years: Dr. Jack Daniel's." His motto, he said, was "I hate people."

"I'd lost everything," Beck recounted later. "I'd lost my money. I'd lost my fancy car. And I was about to lose my family."

Beck says he became a "dry drunk"—he quit drinking, went through the DTs, but continued the behavior of an alcoholic even as he attended Alcoholics Anonymous meetings in a church basement in Cheshire. This went on for a few years, until he was rescued—by his future wife, Tania, and by the prophet Moroni.

Beck met Tania in the parking lot of the radio station; she had come to pick up a Walkman she had won in a contest. At about this time, Beck was heading back to the bottle. "I couldn't hold my alcoholism," he said in tearful testimony to an audience of Mormons. He prayed to God that by "this Thursday, if you don't put a roadblock in my way, I'm going to drink. I cannot walk alone anymore." Beck described how he went to the bar, ordered a Jack and Coke, and "I pick it up and I'm about to drink it and I turn around . . . there across the room is Tania." They left the bar—for coffee.

About a year later, the two were considering marriage, but Tania, a Catholic, told him, "We don't have a faith—I can't marry you." Tania, Beck, and his two daughters went on a church tour, ending up (reluctantly, in Beck's telling) at a Mormon church to appease a longtime Mormon friend and colleague. His decision was clinched when his daughter Mary told him, "I want to go back there." They were baptized in 1999 and married three months later.

"The guy firing people because of the Sharpie was dead and buried," Beck proclaimed. "Where I was only focused on money, booze, business, and cars, I now only wanted to focus on family and people."

Well, maybe not "only" family and people. His conversion gave a big boost to his business—a development Beck describes as miraculous. In Beck's tearful retelling of the moment cited earlier, he was called "out of the blue" by an agent the day after he was baptized. The agent had just told Beck that he should speak to Gabe Hobbs, a Mormon executive with Clear Channel radio—when Hobbs himself called on the other line. Hobbs got him an afternoon talk show in Tampa—a big boost in his visibility and a change in format from music to talk that would launch him to stardom.

An account Beck gave *Forbes* magazine, however, tells a less miraculous tale that has nothing to do with the baptism. In this version, Beck already had the offer from Tampa: "In the late 1990s [Beck is fuzzy on dates], while filling in as a talk-radio host at WABC in New York City, Beck got a lucky call from media agent George Hiltzik, who had been tipped off by the program director. Beck told him he had an offer to do talk radio in Tampa."

As for Beck's "focus on family," he moved to Tampa and left his kids behind in Connecticut with their mother. When callers to his show criticized him for leaving eleven-year-old Mary (his daughter who has cerebral palsy) and eight-year-old Hannah, he pronounced that criticism "over the line." Beck told the *St. Petersburg Times* at the time that "I beat myself up enough for that."

He wondered on air if he'd made a mistake leaving his children, but he evidently decided he had not. Seven years later, he said he was still trying to "visit them regularly." In the meantime, he had two more children with Tania: a daughter, Cheyenne, and an adopted son named Raphe.

Beck admired the inner peace of the Mormons. "I want to be like that," he said. Yet the Mormons weren't entirely sure they wanted him. According to the *Deseret News*: "When Beck was to be ordained into the LDS priesthood, his name was presented to the congregation for a sustaining vote, as is customary in the church. In a highly unusual occurrence, one man opposed the ordination, later telling local leaders, 'Have you heard his show?'"

"I agreed with him," Beck admitted in one of his more candid moments. He worried that his on-air antics would make people "think that's the way Mormons are." Added Beck: "I do stuff on the show every day that I regret or question. My language is loose. I'm just different. Every day I get off the air, I think, 'Lord, help me be better. How do I balance this and be a good reflection of you?' I don't think I hit it very often."

But what he does do very often is employ the story of his redemption and his family to make a point on television and radio.

At the Conservative Political Action Conference, he proposed a twelve-step program for Republicans: "I'm a recovering alcoholic. I screwed up my life six ways to Sunday and I believe in redemption. But the first step to getting redemption is you've got to admit you've got a problem . . . 'Hello, my name is the Republican Party, and I've got a problem. I'm addicted to spending and big government.'"

After Democrats lost some off-year elections, Beck said of President Obama: "As a recovering alcoholic, may I say

I recognize denial? . . . It's like coming to in the bathroom on the floor, naked, for like the fifteenth day in a row." Beck also found in his addiction the laissez-faire wisdom of the free market: "I can tell you with certainty, if no one allowed me to fail, if there were no consequences for my actions, if I kept my family, my job, my house, my wealth, everything else, I wouldn't be able to stop drinking."

Beck's special-needs daughter, too, provides a common Beck touchstone—perseverance. He had been told that Mary, who had several strokes at the time of her birth, would never "walk or talk or feed herself. She went to college. They were wrong," Beck exulted one night on Fox. Another time, he described how Mary ran cross-country in high school and finished "in last place every single race she ran," but still she "completed every race."

Why the constant references to his addictions and his daughter's struggles? He seems to feel his honesty about personal struggles gives him moral authority—and immunity to whatever else might be alleged about him. "I will always tell you the truth, even when it hurts me personally," he told his Fox viewers. By contrast, he said, "The left has already doctored photos, documents, Web sites, which frankly only dishonored them and hurt my children. But as I said to my kids this week, there's more to come."

Beck said those words in early September 2009. Soon after, he took legal action to shut down a Web site called

GlennBeckRapedAndMurderedAYoungGirlIn1990.com. The site was a tasteless spoof of Beck's spurious style of attack: Broadcast an outrageous allegation, qualify it by saying "I'm just asking the question," and then assume it to be true because the victim of the attack doesn't deny it. The joke was that if Beck refused to deny that he had raped and murdered a young girl twenty years ago, then, according to Beck's own formula, it must be true.

Beck, departing from his usual sense of self-awareness, filed a complaint with the World Intellectual Property Organization—an agency of the United Nations, which Beck routinely demonizes as part of a world-government conspiracy. The conspiratorial UN body ruled (naturally) against Beck and in favor of the man who set up the spoof Web site, Florida computer programmer Isaac Eiland-Hall.

Having made his point—and, as a bonus, having lured Beck into acknowledging the authority of the United Nations—the satirist let Beck have the domain name.

CHAPTER 3
THE WHITE HORSE PROPHECY

* *

In one of his first appearances on Fox News—two months before he would start his own show—Glenn Beck sent a coded message to the nation's six million Mormons—or at least those Mormons who believe in what the Latter-day Saints call "the White Horse Prophecy."

"We are at the place where the Constitution hangs in the balance," Beck told Bill O'Reilly on November 14, 2008, just after Obama's election. "I feel the Constitution is hanging in the balance right now, hanging by a thread unless the good Americans wake up."

The Constitution is hanging by a thread.

Most Americans would have heard this as just another bit of overblown commentary and thought nothing more of it. But to those familiar with the White Horse Prophecy, it was an unmistakable signal.

The phrase is often attributed to the Prophet Joseph Smith, founder of the Church of Jesus Christ of Latter-day Saints, or Mormon Church. Smith is believed to have said in 1840 that when the Constitution hangs by a thread, elders of the Mormon Church will step in to save the country.

"When the Constitution of the United States hangs, as it were, upon a single thread, they will have to call for the 'Mormon' Elders to save it from utter destruction; and they will step forth and do it," Brigham Young, Smith's successor as head of the church, wrote in 1855.

Was it just a coincidence in wording, or was Beck, a 1999 Mormon convert, speaking in coded language about the need to fulfill the Mormon prophecy? A conversation on Beck's radio show ten days earlier would seem to rule out coincidence. Beck was interviewing Senator Orrin Hatch of Utah, also a Mormon, when he said: "I heard Barack Obama talk about the Constitution and I thought, we are at the point or we are very near the point where our Constitution is hanging by a thread."

"Well, let me tell you something," Hatch responded. "I believe the Constitution is hanging by a thread."

Days after Beck's Fox show started in January 2009, he had Hatch on, and again prompted him: "I believe our Constitution hangs by a thread."

Hatch concurred.

Large numbers of Mormons watch Beck, but likely

an even larger number of his viewers and radio listeners are evangelical Protestants who have no idea that Beck is preaching to them nightly the theology of the Latter-day Saints.

* * *

There is no way to know how sincerely Glenn Beck holds his views. But we do know that he came to these views recently. He has told us that he was a blank slate before his 1999 conversion to Mormonism. "I didn't know what was really happening in the world," he has said, and "I really didn't care." And, after intense study of the faith, he emerged with the writings of a deceased Mormon thinker—John Birch Society supporter Cleon Skousen—serving as the foundation of his newly acquired worldview.

"I remember, I used to be—believe it or not—a liberal," Beck confessed to viewers one night. "I used to be a social liberal and everything else, but I was a fiscal conservative. Then I discovered alcoholism, and discovered AA, and sobered up. The only way that I knew I could stay sober is if I figured out what I really believe . . . I was never consistent on anything. Unless we're consistent, I don't think we can solve any problem."

Beck found consistency in Mormon theology—which he studied so fervently that he frustrated church leaders: "At one point I had the bishop with his head in his hands, saying 'Glenn, I don't have the answer to that question. I don't think the president of our church has ever been asked that question,'" Beck writes in his book *The Real America*. "I took these through the ringer. Within a month I had exhausted the resources of Mormon.org and had moved on to *Mormon Doctrine*, a book more akin to scholarly use than light reading . . . I like scientific thinking, and I wanted it all to fall into line. For me to join, it needed to logically work and bear good fruit."

The fruit it bore was a philosophy—broadcast on radio and television—that is strikingly similar to the White Horse Prophecy of Joseph Smith.

Before the Mormons went west, Smith traveled to Washington seeking help for his oppressed followers and received nothing but frustration. Rather than turning on the government, however, "They considered themselves the last Real Americans, the legitimate heirs of the pilgrims and Founding Fathers," Pat Bagley writes in the *Salt Lake Tribune*. "And, they believed, the very survival of the Constitution depended on the Saints. From Smith on, LDS leaders prophesied the Constitution would one day hang by a thread, only to be saved by Mormons."

A compilation of church leaders' statements over the years by the journal *BYU Studies* shows this strain of thinking. Though there are doubts about whether Smith actually wrote the phrase "hang by a thread," his successors left no doubt about the theology behind it. Orson Hyde, a Smith contemporary, wrote that Smith believed that "the time would come when the Constitution and the country would be in danger of an overthrow; and said [Smith]: 'If the Constitution be saved at all, it will be by the elders of this Church.'" The church's fifth leader, Charles Nibley, believed that "the day would come when there would be so much of disorder, of secret combinations taking the law into their own hands, tramping upon Constitutional rights and the liberties of the people, that the Constitution would hang as by a thread. Yes, but it will still hang, and there will be enough of good people, many who may not belong to our Church at all, people who have respect for law and for order, and for Constitutional rights, who will rally around with us and save the Constitution."

The prophecy was renewed with each generation of church leadership. "The prophet Joseph Smith said the time will come when, through secret organizations taking the law into their own hands . . . the Constitution of the United States would be so torn and rent asunder, and life and property and peace and security would be held of so little value, that the Constitution would, as it were, hang by a thread," church apostle Melvin Ballard said in 1928. "This Constitution will be preserved, but it will be preserved very largely in consequence of what the Lord has revealed and what this people, through listening to the Lord and being obedient, will help to bring about, to stabilize and give permanency and effect to the Constitution itself. That also is our mission."

And now Beck's mission. Secret organizations? Tramping on liberties? Breakdown of law and order? Shredding the Constitution? Betraying the Founders? This is the core of Beck's message, in his own words: "Some people in the government seem to have a problem, you know, shredding the Constitution. You're trying to protect and defend the Constitution of the United States, friends. It's in trouble . . ." They are "going to bring us to the verge of shredding the Constitution, of massive socialism . . . They see the government as violating the Constitution, and they will see themselves as defenders of the Constitution. Not a good mix. Then they take matters into their own hands."

★ ★ ★

Beck has often described himself as a mere jester. "I'm basically a rodeo clown just trying to entertain you every night," he's been known to say. For most of his career, as a morning-zoo radio DJ, he was nothing more than that.

"We told our bosses right up front: We don't need gimmicks to sell the new Y95," Beck says at the start of a 1986 TV promo for his Phoenix radio show featuring "the new Y95's zookeepers." After a toy airplane flies by, Beck offers "plenty of easy contests for you to win lots of free money."

Cash falls from the ceiling and a stuffed bird swings on a rope. As he and his cohost continue, balloons fall from the ceiling, a live monkey swings onto the set, walks onto the desk, and sips coffee, and a mannequin falls from the ceiling. "Hey, with all that talk on the new Y95, who needs gimmicks?" Beck asks.

The closest he got to substance was offering listeners "your favorite love songs and chances to qualify for a dream trip to Hawaii" (that was on Washington's WPGC). "Twelve before nine—it's 8:48 with the A-Team," he said on a typical Louisville morning on WRKA. "We've been asking you to call us up and tell us who do you think has more class, the fans of U of K or the fans of U of L?"

If Beck had any trace, back then, of his current persona, it was his delight in causing offense. In New Haven, he and his partner made fun of Asian Americans, using a mock accent; the *Hartford Advocate* reported that the station had to apologize. (The ethnic games have continued. As recently as 2003, he had this to say of Barbra Streisand in his *Real America* book: "Sometimes I just feel like screaming, 'Shut up, you big-nosed cross-eyed freak!' " And of Joe Lieberman: "I know Joe well. Well, we're not buddies or anything, not like we're out buying yarmulkes together.")

Beck made a rare foray into public affairs one morning in 1986 after Reagan ordered the bombing of Libya. He and a friend had written a song with the chorus "Gaddafi

Sucks, Gaddafi Sucks" and Reagan's voice saying "Frankly, Gaddafi sucks" over the New Wave music of the time. Beck was tentative: "I originally didn't want to play it because I felt it was a little too offensive," he said, "but we're going to play it here and we'd like to hear what you think."

The station was flooded with supportive calls. Caller "Eric" said of Libyan terrorists: "We should bring them back to the United States and publicly execute them, probably just slow torture on world TV." Eric further proposed: "Give them a couple alternatives like slide them down, down a, well I'm trying to think, a pool of razor blades filled with alcohol. Slowly lower them into a pool of piranhas."

Beck was mild in his response. "Thank you Eric, appreciate it, bye-bye," he said to the angry man. But he had learned that he had the power to rile. "I just want to say, I feel really good," he said as he signed off the air that morning.

When, in the 1990s, he moved to Connecticut—where he crashed, sobered up, changed wives, and found religion—Beck was searching for an ideology beyond that of the morning zoo. With the help of Senator Joe Lieberman, a Connecticut Democrat, Beck, then a supporter of abortion rights who wore his hair in a ponytail, enrolled in a religion class at Yale. It was, he recalled, titled "Early Christology: The Making of the Image of Christ." At the same time, he endeavored to have books replace drinks in his life: He went to bookstores and assembled "the library of a serial killer," including titles by Alan Dershowitz, the pope, Nietzsche, Hitler, Carl Sagan, Billy Graham, Plato, and Kant.

As he read philosophy and searched for a church, Beck began to adopt a more conservative persona, on air and off. During the Bill Clinton impeachment proceedings of late 1998 and early 1999, he gave his patron Lieberman a copy of John F. Kennedy's *Profiles in Courage* to encourage him to vote to convict Clinton. "He was offended," Beck later recalled. "That was the last time we ever spoke."

Beck's conversion to Mormonism in 1999 coincided with a whole new level of conservative positions. By now he had short hair and at some point along the way acquired what he calls his "relatively new" position of being "staunchly pro-life." But he didn't embrace all of the Mormon customs, such as those involving foul language. While still at KC101 in Connecticut a month after his baptism, he hurled obscenities on air at a caller who complained about "people like you and Rush Limbaugh talking about morality and you have none." Beck told her, "You don't give a crap about the truth" and called her an "evil little bitch."

Beck finally got what he wanted in 2000: a chance to follow radio successes such as Limbaugh into an all-talk format. He got an afternoon radio spot in Tampa and was soon nationally syndicated. Then, as now, his format was about public affairs but often had nothing to do with the news of the day. Writing in 2003 about attending a talk-radio convention, he recalled being bored by the topics the others were talking about: taxes, prescription drugs, party politics, and the presidential campaign. "Does anybody want to hang out with anybody who is excited by that collection of Jack Kevorkian, auto-suicidal C-SPAN material?" Beck asked. "If you can't interest a roomful of talk-show hosts in partisan politics, you certainly can't get somebody who lives in Omaha, Nebraska, and works at the Dunkin' Donuts to listen to it."

No, Beck knew that he needed something more dramatic than the news of the day. To become really big in the talk business, he didn't need to inform his audience. He needed to entertain them, anger them, frighten them. And he found what he needed in his new church.

★ ★ ★

On the morning of July 16, 2009, Beck was on the air for his radio show when he asked his producer, not for the first time, "Can you get the Ezra Taft Benson quote for me?" For listeners, he identified Benson as Dwight Eisenhower's secretary of agriculture. He did not disclose that Benson was also the thirteenth president of the Mormon Church, who died five years before Beck's baptism.

Beck played the audio of Benson recounting a conversation with Khrushchev in which the Soviet leader told him:

"You Americans are so gullible. No, you won't accept communism outright, but we'll keep feeding you small doses of socialism until you'll finally wake up and find you already have communism."

Beck developed Benson's views into a cornerstone of his own philosophy as he waged war against "progressives" trying to sneak communism into America "step by step," as he puts it. "Progressivism says, 'Bit by bit we'll eat at the Constitution,'" Beck informed his viewers. Another day, he described the progressive plan "to rot America from the inside . . . make progress, baby steps."

At the Conservative Political Action Conference in Washington, he asked the audience, "What's the difference" between a communist and a progressive? "Well, there's no difference except one requires a gun and the other does it slowly, piece by piece, eating away at it," Beck explained, channeling Benson.

★ ★ ★

Beck's embrace of Mormon political thinkers actually begins with a Roman Catholic: the late Carroll Quigley, Bill Clinton's mentor at Georgetown University. An otherwise reputable academic, Quigley became celebrated among conspiracy types for a brief passage in his 1966 tome, *Tragedy & Hope*, in which he described the workings of the so-called Round Table Group.

"There does exist, and has existed for a generation, an international Anglophile network," he wrote. He described a web of organizations including the Council on Foreign Relations and J.P. Morgan & Co., and said that "this elaborate, semi-secret organization" aimed to "coordinate the international activities," and had behind it "the power of the international financial coterie."

Quigley's words, which get some credit for launching the One World Government conspiracy, inspired many conspiracy theorists who came to influence Beck's views quite directly. But Quigley's original allegation had an effect on Beck as well.

"Let me take you back to right after 9/11," Beck told his viewers one night. "I was a really lazy American. I didn't know much about American history. I didn't know anything about anything really . . . I started to read everything I could get my hands on. One of the books I found was this one, *Tragedy & Hope*."

Beck said Quigley had "a better idea than the doomsday device or MAD" (the cold-war nuclear strategy of mutually assured destruction). "Instead of tying everybody to a master computer that showed that we're going to blow everything up, they decided to tie everybody's economies together . . . Mutually assured economic destruction, OK? No weapons involved—just money, tie it all together."

Another time, Beck told radio listeners: "I know it's not

popular to quote Carroll Quigley but if you've ever read *Tragedy & Hope* from the 1960s, you see this being played out." And what was being "played out"? There exists, he argued, a "shadow government" in which the Democratic and Republican parties are identical, both secondary to the "companies taking over and really controlling everything."

Interesting. But this resembles not in the least what Quigley was describing. Rather, Beck had embraced an interpretation of Quigley—a misinterpretation, Quigley himself said—by Cleon Skousen, who wrote a book, *The Naked Capitalist*, based on Quigley's *Tragedy & Hope*. "Skousen is apparently a political agitator. I am an historian," Quigley protested in a Mormon journal called *Dialogue*. Quigley had described a loose international organization aimed at improving economies; Skousen turned this into a nefarious plot to control the world. Beck embraced the latter.

Actually, Beck had embraced all things Skousen—particularly a book he had written called *The 5,000 Year Leap*, asserting that the Founders were moved by biblical law to write the Constitution. Skousen's nephew Mark Skousen appeared on Beck's show and recounted the episode in the conservative magazine *Human Events*:

"Last Friday, Beck passed out to the live audience a new edition of *The 5,000 Year Leap*, with an introduction by him. He told the audience, 'Everyone should read this book.' Between commercials, he told me that even though he had never met my uncle (he died in 2006), Cleon's book changed his life. He said that a friend, without solicitation, sent him a copy of *The 5,000 Year Leap*, saying, 'Glenn, I don't know if you've ever read this, but it's the simplest, easiest way for Americans of all ages to understand the simple yet brilliant principles our founders based this country on.' Glenn read the book, and concluded: 'The author was years ahead of his time. And our founders were thousands of years ahead of their time. My hope is that all Americans young and old will spend the time with this book to understand why we are who we are. The words of our Founding Fathers have a way of reaching across any political divide. They are words of wisdom that I can only describe as divinely inspired.'"

Beck pitched the book in his radio and TV shows. His promotion of *The 5,000 Year Leap* pushed the book, after three decades in obscurity, to number one in the Amazon .com rankings. Few could have known much about the author of the book they were all buying.

Skousen, an ally of the far-right John Birch Society, had been a cold-war communist hunter. He regarded *The Manchurian Candidate* not as a fictional movie but as a documentary. A Brigham Young University professor, he reacted to pressure on the Mormon Church to ordain blacks as priests by declaring that communists were attacking the Mormons.

Eventually, the head of the Mormon Church issued an

edict to churches to "avoid any implication that the Church endorses what is said" by Skousen's movement. But Skousen's movement (it changed its name from the Freemen Institute to the National Center for Constitutional Studies after militia groups began to use the "freemen" label) persisted. Skousen, claiming to represent the beliefs of the Founding Fathers, called for the abolition of Social Security, farm subsidies, and education and welfare funding; pulling out of the United Nations; and eliminating federal income taxes and most federal regulatory agencies.

Skousen's ideas might have died with him, but all that changed when Beck turned *The 5,000 Year Leap* into his manifesto.

Skousen, at the start of the book, includes a diagram of the political spectrum stretching from "anarchy" to "tyranny." Beck draws the very same diagram on his chalkboard, though he substitutes "total government" for "tyranny."

"Measuring people and issues in terms of political parties has turned out to be philosophically fallacious," Skousen wrote. "Communism and Fascism turned out to be different names for approximately the same thing—the police state." Skousen argued that "the American founders considered the two extremes to be ANARCHY on the one hand, and TYRANNY on the other." He wrote that the original Articles of Confederation were "too close to anarchy."

Compare this to Beck, using the Skousen diagram on his chalkboard: "Fascism and communism are the same," he said in March 2010. "It's total anarchy that is on this end. Here's the republic, here's a progressive government that leads you to either fascism or communism." Another night, Beck gestures to the "tyranny" end of the drawing: "This here is fascism, communism, statism. This is total complete control by the government." He gestures to the other side. "This is anarchy here." He tells viewers that the "Articles of Confederation . . . was as close to this line to anarchy as we could possibly get."

Alas, Skousen's—and therefore Beck's—view of the Founders' intent is a bit creative. Skousen's book, for example, has a section titled "The Founders Warn Against the Drift Toward the Collectivist Left." As evidence of this warning, he uses a quote from Jefferson: "If we can prevent the government from wasting the labors of the people, under the pretense of taking care of them, they must become happy."

But Skousen neglects to mention that the quote was part of an argument Jefferson was having with his rivals in the Federalist Party. They, too, were Founders, and they argued the other side: that government should be stronger. Then, as now, the proper size of government was fiercely debated.

Likewise, Skousen supplies a quotation from Benjamin Franklin "emphasizing the importance of marriage as he attempted to dissuade a young friend from taking a mistress." He quotes Franklin: "Marriage is the proper remedy. It is the most natural state of man, and therefore the state in which you are most likely to find solid happiness."

But Skousen doesn't quote from the rest of the same Franklin letter, in which he argues that it is better to take older women as mistresses because "they are so grateful," because "they are more prudent and discreet," and because "the compunction is less." Writes Franklin: "As in the dark all cats are gray, the pleasure of corporal enjoyment with an old woman is at least equal, and frequently superior, every knack being by practice capable of improvement."

Skousen's history was heavily doctored, but it gave Beck a template. He took up the cause of the late Skousen. He started "Founders' Fridays" on his Fox show to preach this selective reading of history. His goal: to restore America to the fanciful state, invented by Skousen, in which all of the Founding Fathers support Beck's worldview.

"Tonight," he said at the beginning of one Founders' Friday, "we want to do revisionist history." He proposed to "show you some of the examples of where history is just wrong."

He began with George Washington, father of our country, understood through history to be, like many other Founders, a Deist—a believer in a noninterventionist God. Not so, Beck announced. "Washington was just a die-hard Christian."

He brought in Peter Lillback, president of the Westminster Theological Seminary, to prove it. "He had a vibrant personal Anglican or Episcopalian Christian faith," Lillback confirmed. But this has been hidden by a generations-long conspiracy by secular historians! "A devout evangelical Christian Founding Father didn't play well for those that wanted to move beyond Christian influence," Lillback alleged.

Lillback went on to argue that "a form of historical revisionism" has required people to take the elevator to the top of the Washington Monument rather than the stairs. Sure, the Parks Service may say it's because of safety and crowd control, but Lillback thinks it's really because the stairwells contain "scriptural messages."

"I can't prove this, but I've heard that there is a copy of the top of the Washington Monument that's on display in a museum in Washington, but it has been carefully turned so you can't see the Latin words" meaning "Glory to God," Lillback went on to assert. "I heard that said so many times, it must be true."

Now *that's* academic rigor.

An honest discussion of the view of the Founders as die-hard Christians might have addressed the words of Thomas Paine, whom, in other contexts, Beck has celebrated as a champion of liberty. "I do not believe in the creed professed by the Jewish Church, by the Roman Church, by the Greek Church, by the Turkish Church, by the Protestant Church, nor by any church that I know of," Paine wrote in *The Age of Reason*. "My own mind is my own church."

Instead, Beck went to his next guest, historian Burton Folsom, to talk about how bad men such as Woodrow Wilson and Barack Obama are undoing the good work of religious conservatives such as George Washington. "A lot of people would speculate that maybe Barack Obama has a little contempt for history of America or western civilization," Beck proposed. "Do you see a pattern or a similarity between the two of them [Wilson and Obama] in that?"

Folsom did see a pattern (he must have wanted to be invited back to Beck's show). Wilson and Obama "don't share any kind of respect, deep respect for the Constitution," he said. "Wilson thought it was outmoded and so does Barack Obama."

"Right," Beck concurred. "They don't necessarily hate it, but it's just that it was a nice thing in the past."

"It worked in 1776, but today we can trust leaders with more power," Folsom said.

The Constitution is hanging by a thread. As Beck views it, he alone speaks for the Founders, and "there's no sidelines here. You're either on the side of the revolutionaries for Marxism and a new Venezuela here in America, or the revolutionaries of 1776." Mormon conspiracy theories may provide good entertainment for millions, but there is at least one group that isn't amused. A number of Mormon scholars at Brigham Young got together to hold a panel discussion titled "Glenn Beck, Cleon Skousen and LDS Conservatism." The session was written up in the *Deseret News*.

"He's just throwing stuff out there," political science professor Ralph Hancock said. In both Skousen and Beck, Hancock said, "I find . . . a trace of anti-intellectualism. My interest is to help connect a certain LDS conservative impulse or mood with a more deeply grounded intellectual conservatism." Hancock, the newspaper reported, told the Mormon students in the audience that rather than going Beck's route, they should "study diligently to increase our confidence that our intense feelings are common sense and can be rationally articulated." The professor urged "alternatives to the kind of proof-texting, quote-listing approach," such as "literature that is more substantial and sound."

Soundness and substance? That's death for ratings.

CHAPTER 4

THE END IS NEAR . . . AND THE RATINGS ARE THROUGH THE ROOF!

. . . .

"Three, two, one—Beck!"

The announcer's voice, introducing Beck's show in his first months on Fox News, suggested that something was about to explode. Invariably, it did.

"Come on, let's go!" the cherubic entertainer invites, and the performance is under way. He whispers. He shouts. He bounces from his knees and waves his arms wildly. He puts his hand to his mouth and pauses to gather his thoughts and reflect on the gravity of the situation. He calls himself just "a regular schmo" who's asking questions.

But the questions, shouts, and whispers all point in one direction: The End Is Near.

"I haven't verbalized what I think is coming next because I think it's horrific. I think what's coming is horrific," he tells us on the radio. "I don't even want to speak it out loud.

I've said it to my wife; she sat up in the bed for quite a while and just kind of couldn't get her arms around it. I hope I'm wrong. I pray that I'm wrong."

And: "You've got to be off this ship. You've got to build lifeboats. You got to prepare your family."

And: "These bills are creating the path to America's destruction! They are building a machine and they're about to turn the darn thing on! You don't compromise on your destruction."

And: "I think we are headed for extraordinarily dangerous times. I think we are . . . headed—we're headed toward civil unrest. God knows what. Please, America—please, keep things under control and look at Martin Luther King and Gandhi as an example."

And: "The country may not survive Barack Obama . . . If he does fundamentally transform America, we're done. You don't have to worry about a 2012."

Seldom does a night pass without a dire warning such as "our very country is at stake," or perhaps even an illustration of the calamity. "So, here are the three scenarios that we could be facing," he tells viewers one evening. "Recession, depression, or collapse." He writes the three possibilities on his chalkboard, in case it wasn't clear.

Well, thank you, Mr. Beck, and have a nice doomsday.

Of all the strains running through Beck's brain—philosophical, historical, and sometimes paranoid—the apocalyptic strain seems to be the most enduring. Though he has come only lately to his view that "progressivism" is the source of all evil, he has long promoted a vision of doom that, by design or coincidence, fits neatly with the End Times views of many of his fundamentalist viewers.

For Fox News viewers new to Beck's end-of-the-world thinking, he held a special show on the subject a month after arriving. It was called "Faith and Survival; Surviving the Unthinkable."

The program even came with a disclaimer at the start: "Warning: Topics discussed on today's program may be disturbing to some viewers. The views expressed in this program are not predictions of what will happen, but what could happen. The panelists have been asked to think the unthinkable. Viewer discretion is advised."

For the night, Beck turned his set into "the war room" and proposed to "play out some of the worst-case scenarios." Promised Beck: "We're going to try to show you how to prepare for the worst while everybody else is sitting back and hoping for the best."

"The truth is," he said with high drama, over what he later called "spooky" music, "that you are the defender of liberty."

Here are the scenarios Beck laid out for his defenders of liberty, all occurring in the year 2014:

1. "All the U.S. banks have been nationalized. Unemployment is about between 12 percent and 20 percent. Dow is trading at 2,800. The real estate market has collapsed. Government and unions control most of the business, and America's credit rating has been downgraded."

2. "Global civil unrest. Now, the United States is no longer the world's policeman. Mexico has been taken over by narco gangs. Oil and gas pipelines have been targeted and destroyed. Tourism nonexistent due to safety concerns."

3. "Anger and discontent at home. The year is 2014. Many Americans are feeling disenfranchised. People are isolated from their political leaders and have been betrayed over and over and over again. Internet connects like-minded people and the 'Bubba Effect'—a rise in individual militias."

One guest, Gerald Celente of the Trends Research Institute, elaborated: "New York City looks like Mexico City . . . We're going to see major cities look like Calcutta. There is going to be the homeless, panhandlers, hookers."

Don't forget hyperinflation, Beck added. "Money is, in our scenario . . . really worthless . . . People make their own money." He then stepped back from the hypothetical and showed his audience a "Liberty Dollar," a counterfeit "barter" currency that had been circulated in Indiana. Federal authorities had arrested various people in connection with distributing the silver and gold coins, but Beck was encouraging the counterfeiters on national television.

Beck resumed his war gaming, announcing that there would be no more Social Security and no government. "Nothing is safe," said Beck.

Beck then proposed to start growing his own food, saying, "I worry about my kids."

Another guest, retired military man Tim Strong, described a "survivalist attitude" of communities fending for themselves.

"That's like a 'Mad Max' community," Beck observed, later adding that the results would at the very least be "disenfranchisement and a possible uprising here in the United States."

They spoke about war in the Middle East and 95 percent tax rates.

"Tax revolts," said Beck.

"This is going to be violent," added Celente. "The cities are going to look like Dodge City. They're going to be uncontrollable. You're going to have gangs in control, motorcycle marauders." (Celente had earlier offered viewers the Web site of a survival combat trainer, AttackProof .com.)

"This is the scenario that would tear this country apart,

and spiral us into something that maybe we have never even seen before, including the Civil War," Beck declared. "This scenario scares the living daylights out of me because it is completely—it is shaking nitroglycerine."

Apparently the host wasn't the only one who had the living daylights scared out of him. Beck had encouraged a new wave of survivalists planning for the apocalypse. Something called the "Survival Seed Bank" began advertising on Beck's show.

"Are you worried about the economy?" a man asks at the beginning of a commercial for the company, which at first sounds like a Beck parody. "Have you ever wondered if the politicians and the bankers are going to bring the whole thing crashing down? If so, pay close attention. Because in an economic meltdown, non-hybrid seeds could become more valuable than even silver and gold."

The commercial shows Depression-era footage of breadlines. "After all," the narrator continues, "securing a source of food for your family is the single most important thing you can do." Cut to a scene of the man bringing a basket of vegetables into his kitchen. "Introducing the Survival Seed Bank," he says. "The perfect mix of germination-tested non-hybrid seeds. You get enough seeds to plant a full-acre crisis garden. Remember: In a real economic crisis, non-hybrid seeds are the ultimate barter item."

On the Illinois business's Web site, the bank is offered

for $149 plus $15 for shipping and handling ("for the general public, the price will be a fat $297" with "no discounts, even to FEMA or military personnel") by calling a toll-free number. "Indestructible Survival Seed Bank Can Be Buried to Avoid Confiscation," the Web site boasts.

Other Beck advertisers include a provider of power generators and gold dealers.

As with other parts of Beck's message, there are similarities between his doomsday theories and Mormon theology. The prophet Joseph Smith, in his Articles of Faith, writes of a messianic age headquartered in the United States: "We believe in the literal gathering of Israel and in the restoration of the Ten Tribes; that Zion (the New Jerusalem) will be built upon the American continent; that Christ will reign personally upon the earth; and, that the earth will be renewed and receive its paradisiacal glory."

But Beck is so conversant with End Times theory that he also frequently brings in Muslim doomsday prophecies on his show. His favorite: "The Twelvers."

"Iranian President Mahmoud Ahmadinejad—this guy is a Twelver," Beck told his viewers one night. "Not a 9/12er"—those are Beck's followers—"a Twelver . . . You're looking for the Twelfth Imam. It's a radical Twelver. They were so radical they were banned by the Ayatollah Khomeini for being cuckoo."

Beck outlined their views: "You need to cause global

chaos, because only in global chaos will the Mahdi come, so they believe that by blowing stuff up and starting wars and having global bloodshed, the promised one will come sooner."

The theme returned on another show. "When President Ahmadinejad says he wants to vaporize Israel, he's not trying to trick people, it's not a power bluff. He believes he's fulfilling prophecy," Beck explained. "What prophecy? This is—I'm not a theologian." But he plays one on TV.

He offered to explain it "off the top of my head," and he put it in terms he knew his audience would understand: the Book of Revelation.

"If you are a Christian, you know the world is washed in blood and Jesus comes back and splits the mountains," he explained. "Theirs is very, very similar. The promised one comes—the Twelfth Imam comes and has to wash the world in blood . . . See if this sounds familiar to Christians. This would be the tribulation. Global government in Babylon. If you are a Christian, who is setting up the global government in Babylon? That would be the Antichrist. Who's doing it? According to the Twelvers, the promised one."

Another night, he brought on a guest to analyze this news. "So the Mahdi, when he comes crawling out of the well, he is supposed to create a global government. He persecutes the Christians and he has them either submit or he cuts their heads off, right?"

"Right," replied the guest. "In fact, what's more, the Islamic messiah is supposed to come with Jesus."

"He'll testify to the Mahdi and he'll say, 'Hey, by the way, you guys misunderstood. I'm not the son of God. This is the man right here.' Correct?" Beck inquired.

"Right," said the guest.

"They seem to me to be a lot like End Times prophecy," Beck observed.

"It's a mirror image," the guest replied.

The difference: Beck only promotes the Christian version on his show. "I'm not saying these things are true," he said, offering his usual qualifier after floating a conspiracy. "But it's important that you understand this."

Beck has been dabbling in (or, depending on your perspective, exploiting) End Times faith for several years. In 2006, he led off his CNN Headline News show with word that August 22 "is the day that Israel might be wiped off the map leading to all-out Armageddon."

"What I'm about to tell you nobody else is going to tell you," he said of his "World War III" hypothesis. "Honestly, it gave me great pause today, because it's verging on the edge of insanity. It really is. With that being said, the source is so good there's no way I can't tell you this news."

He attributed it to a Princeton professor predicting that "Islamic End of Times prophecies could be fulfilled" in a mere fortnight. More evidence: There are "eleven miss-

ing Egyptians with no visas" on the loose in America.
"You've got to put the political correctness aside and let me
show their frickin' pictures on television," he demanded.
"We're fighting not only for the existence of our country,
but . . . possibly the existence of the entire planet."

August 22, 2006, came and went without incident.

But the next year, Beck was back, interviewing a conservative pastor by the name of John Hagee, whose
anti-Catholic views became an embarrassment for John
McCain's presidential campaign.

"We're living in the End Times—you believe that?" Beck
asked.

"I do indeed," Hagee answered. "The Bible is very
specific to the fact." He then walked Beck through the
prophecies.

"Is the Antichrist alive today?" Beck inquired.

"I believe he is," Hagee answered.

"End of the world as we know it in five years, ten years,
twenty years?"

"I don't think we'll get past twenty years."

"Putin, is he part of the biblical prophecy?"

"I believe that he's the man that's going to cause Russia
to unite the Islamic nations against Israel."

"What TV show would Jesus watch?"

"He probably wouldn't."

"Wrong answer," Beck informed the minister.

"Glenn Beck!" Hagee corrected.

Not long after that interview, Beck posted an article on his Web site titled " 'Doomsday' Seed Vault Opens in Arctic." Europeans were storing seed samples inside a Norwegian mountain in case global warming destroyed crops.

In one show, he brought on an investor who informed viewers that "debt implosion, which is what we're in the process of realizing right now, is potentially even anarchy— anarchy and the society. And so individuals and families have to have the foresight, that situational awareness to perhaps consider, you know, maybe having a farm, maybe growing your own food. Maybe you need to take up arms if you have them and learn to protect your family. The period that's emerging in front of us could be scary, very scary."

"He's spookier than I am," Beck rejoiced.

On and on went prophecies of doom.

On his radio show, he likened the economic situation to a "doomsday device" that guaranteed massive retaliation in a nuclear strike. "Socialist policies have tricked this system into thinking that we have started a war," he told listeners. "Economies are starting to crash."

On a spring evening in May 2010, he likened the state of America to that of the *Titanic*, post-iceberg. "America, this is your third warning now that I've counted. This is the third time I've heard people say we're just buying time," he said. He told them of a quotation that "hungry people fighting over food don't usually make real sound decisions," and recommended, "You have to make yours now."

"This ship, it's sinking now," he continued, explaining his own preparations for the end. "I've been eating fruit all day because I realized—I got news for you, man. A world without cupcakes, I'm dead within two hours. I got to get into shape." He also advised viewers to "turn to God and live."

But they apparently don't have much time left to find God. "Is America going to survive?" he asked his viewers a month before offering them the *Titanic* analogy. "Or are we going to fundamentally transform into something that nobody can describe or identify?" The evidence, in Beck's world, points to the latter outcome.

One night he told viewers that Iranian leaders "are telling their people that these are the End of Days, setting them up for something, and there is something about the Persian Gulf turning blood red, and that is now happening."

The health-care bill, he said, "is the end of America as you know it." The political system, he said, "is corrupt! And if we don't fix it, we're doomed." As things stand now, he said, "We're facing the destruction of our country in the next—I don't even know—one year, five years, ten years. But it's coming—on this course, it's coming."

For one show he even brought out a Jenga building set and began to play with it to illustrate how the system would collapse. "The game that we're playing right now is, how many of these can be taken out?" he continued. "How many of these problems and solutions can you slide out before the whole darn thing collapses?" After he finished the game, he told viewers that "before you know it, the whole thing will collapse . . . It will collapse on you and your family."

When Obama spoke about his cap-and-trade proposal for curbing greenhouse gases, Beck tore away papers pasted to his chalkboard. "You're going to see a black and white world, man, that is nothing but destruction and ugly," he forecast. "I don't know why no one else will tell you the truth about all these things . . . It is only when you take down the mask of sunshine and lollipops that you will see the real thing, the real image: destruction!"

Even Beck had to realize the apocalypse thing was getting a bit too much. One night, after his doomsday talk was mocked by Stephen Colbert, Beck brought his own "fear consultant" onto the show.

"Now, I fully appreciate that you're very worried about expanding government, Islamic fascism, the trampling of the Constitution, economic meltdown, socialistic policies, Mexico, North Korea, Pakistan, End Times, global unrest, Al Franken, street riots, cholesterol, salmon, yada yada," the consultant said.

"I'm actually not trying to be alarming," said Beck.

"No, you need to be more alarming, Glenn. Killer bees! . . . Black holes!"

Alas, there was no stopping the march to Armageddon:

"Your right to keep and bear arms is under attack."

"Your freedom of speech is under attack."

"Our freedom is under attack."

"Our Constitution is under attack."

"Families are under attack."

"Religion is under attack."

"Faith is under attack."

"The entire system is under attack."

"Talk radio is under attack."

"Fox is under attack."

"I'm under attack."

"I think everybody is under attack."

"We're all under attack."

"God is under attack."

"We are under attack in almost every shape and form in America."

Okay, Glenn. We got the idea.

"You know, I know we don't know each other," Beck told his viewers one night, "but I feel like I know you . . . I think you fear for our future."

How couldn't they? They've been watching Glenn Beck.

CHAPTER 5

CRAZY LIKE A FOX

* *

Is Glenn Beck crazy?

The question has been answered in the affirmative by no less an authority than Glenn Beck. He did this while interviewing himself.

"There is a talk-radio host you may have heard of that many blogs around the country said was nearly driven to madness by a caller from Massachusetts, of all places," Beck said on his TV show one evening. "Here he is."

The picture switched to . . . Glenn Beck! In shirtsleeves, doing his radio show.

"Where is your logic?" a caller named Kathy is asking him. "What would you do? I'm asking you, what would you do to change this health-care system for the better? After all, every time you people bring up cost, you don't care about the trillions of dollars to bail out the banks and all the credit card companies."

At this, Beck explodes. "Kathy, get off my phone!" Beck is pumping his arms in the air maniacally. "Get off my phone, you little pinhead! I don't care? You people don't care about the trillions?" Beck slips into a high-pitched screech. "I'm going to lose my mind today," he shrieks.

"That's shameful," the TV version of Beck said when the clip ended. Then, as he announced himself as his official guest, an image of the radio version of Beck appeared on the split screen, wearing a sweatshirt and a "TF" baseball cap for Bill O'Reilly's show, *The Factor*.

"Thank you for finally having somebody who disagrees with you, you know, on the air once in a while," Radio Beck told TV Beck.

"A lot of people say you've lost your mind," TV Beck said to Radio Beck.

"You know, I have lost my mind," Radio Beck said. "You know, what's the difference between me and you, you know what I mean? I've lost my mind. You're a big fat fatty. You're on TV all the time. But yes, I lost my mind. You know, are you watching the news? . . . I mean, the whole country is melting down. People aren't even paying attention."

An understanding TV Beck replied, "And that's why you were screaming 'get off my phone' to that lady because she wasn't paying attention?"

"Yes," Radio Beck volleyed. "I think yelling at people and then hanging up on them is the only real way to save America at this point . . . Doing that to one person every day—it's not enough," Radio Beck continued, explaining that yelling at people should be worked into one's daily routine. "You know, people are picking up a newspaper . . . What, are you crazy? 'Get out of my newspaper!' "

"You're starting to sound a little nuts," TV Beck informed his radio self.

"Oh, I'm starting to sound crazy?" Radio Beck asked, offended.

"Yeah, you are, just a little bit."

"I knew you'd say that," crazy Radio Beck replied. "The magic bean in my pocket told me you would say that. Oh, I know who you are."

TV Beck moved to cut off the madman.

"Get off my screen, you pinhead!" Radio Beck shrieked.

It was pitch-perfect comedy, but the segment also said everything you need to know about Beck's mental state. He may say and do crazy things, but that doesn't mean he's crazy.

There are millions of Americans who fear their government, which usually makes them angry at their government. In Beck, they found somebody who will give voice to their paranoia.

After Poland's president was killed when his plane tried to land in fog in Russia, a caller to Beck's radio show saw something darker. "Call me paranoid," the caller said. (Okay, if you insist.) "I smell a rat in the destruction of the

Polish government on that airplane." The caller thought it might have been a plot by "the Ruskies."

Beck allowed the man to spin the conspiracy theory, then validated it. "I don't put anything past a former KGB agent," he said. "We are dealing with the powers of darkness . . . I don't know if anybody had anything to do with this physically, but I'm telling you we are dealing with the powers of darkness in the world today."

But you don't get three million viewers a night by merely validating existing paranoid delusions; you must also feed the paranoid new things to fret about. This is why Beck tells his viewers and listeners, day after day, that the government is out to get him.

"Even with all the resources of Fox, the truth still can't be fully exposed without you. I ask you, please help us. Meet us here every day," he urged his followers one evening in May 2009. Conspiratorially, he continued, warning about an unspecified "they" and "them": "The status quo is what gives them their status. It is what brings them to power and self-importance. Use your voice while you still have it. I tell you, with everything in me, I think they are going to silence voices like mine and Bill O'Reilly and Rush and everybody else. They will silence us. They can't let us continue to speak out. When the government is trying to influence what kind of syrup a restaurant uses, do you really think they're going to have a problem regulating opinion?"

It was a dark and sinister plot Beck was outlining. But if he truly believed this, he recovered fairly quickly. A moment later, he was telling viewers, "You know what? We're going to do some comedy on the road." He directed them to his Web site for ticket information.

Months later, "they" weren't merely trying to silence him. They were trying to kill him. One night in March 2010, Beck was on a familiar topic, the evils of "social justice," when he argued that the Obama administration and its supporters had violated three of the Ten Commandments: stealing, coveting, and bearing false witness. "And for those of you in the administration who are coming after me on this one—I mean, remember, you've broken three, let's not make it four. Thou shall not kill."

In late May 2010, Beck appeared on Fox Business Network to speak about a plot by the White House and its allies that involved "targeting and destroying" him. "Isolate and destroy. That is their whole mantra. They tried to do it with Rush. They tried to do it with Fox. They're just coming after me. They have been relentless. This kind of stuff is coming after me for over a year."

The host, David Asman, was concerned. "Does it have any effect on you personally, emotionally?"

"No," Beck said, before reconsidering. "When you have your children in jeopardy, which my children have been in jeopardy, when your family is under attack, when you have the death threats, when you can't go anywhere without major security, because of these groups and what they say and how they distort and how they lie, yes, it affects somebody personally. You bet it does."

But brave Beck said he would press on—"until my dying breath."

The problem is, "they" are interested in killing more than just Glenn Beck. "They are building a machine that will crush the entrepreneurial spirit and the freedom that our Founding Fathers designed," Beck warned another day. "This machine, whatever it is they are building, will crush it. Do not let them build another piece. So while I turn away, I want to make sure that I have at least ten million eyes watching—watching every single move they're making."

"They," Beck said at another point, "will gather strength and you will not be able to stand against them . . . They're going inside our government . . . These people are thugs . . . I fear that there will come a time when I cannot say things that I am currently saying."

Beck frequently advises his viewers to fear home invasions. Sometimes these invasions come in the form of parenting advice. "You will have to shoot me in the forehead before I will let you into my house to tell me how to raise my children." Sometimes they are to disarm the population: "You will have to shoot me in the forehead before you take away my gun." Sometimes they are to silence dissent:

"You will have to shoot me in the forehead before I acquiesce and be silent."

Even something as simple as a census questionnaire leads to a home invasion. Beck, refusing to fill out his census form completely, warned those census workers who might come to his door in search of the missing information: "Have a good time trying to get past the dogs and the gates. Enjoy that, enjoy that." Laughing, he added: "I don't suggest you climb over the walls. The dogs are really, really hungry. You've been warned. Don't step on the property. Guard dogs—and other things."

On the air, Beck fancies himself being stalked by those he targets on the show, including former White House adviser Van Jones ("If I'm found dead in the streets it's either Van Jones or Imus," he told radio host Don Imus), the voter registration organization ACORN ("If I'm ever in a weird accident or a suicide or something, after the media's done celebrating, could they check into it?"), and the head of the service employees union ("I hope he doesn't break my legs or have my legs broken").

In the paranoid mind, enemies lurk in every nook and cranny. So, too, on *The Glenn Beck Show*.

One day, Beck informed his followers that he was being "targeted by those who are in the Oval Office with the president."

Another day he said he expects "dogs and firehoses" to

be used against him and his followers. "I wouldn't be surprised if a few of us get a billy club to the head."

Another day, he said they were reading his e-mails. "I do believe the government could be reading mine," he said. "During the Bush administration somebody told me, who would have access to know, I have a file. I can guarantee you I have got a file at least at the White House now."

Terrorist watch list? Gitmo waiting list?

Even automotive safety has been seen as a possible vehicle with which big government could attack Beck. Take the "OnStar" system, which can remotely disable a stolen car's engine. But when the government took ownership in General Motors, this technology acquired a sinister meaning. "Our government is starting to consume everything and control everything," Beck told radio listeners. "Do you want the government to be able to know where you are in your car all the time, also be able to have a microphone in your car?"

On March 9, 2010, Beck had on his TV show the disgraced Democratic congressman Eric Massa, who had just resigned from Congress as allegations emerged of sexual advances he had made on male staffers. Ostensibly, Beck had Massa on to dish dirt on the Democrats, but instead the host wound up vying with his guest in a persecution contest. As Massa tried to outline his troubles, Beck broke in with "bullcrap, sir," using an expression apparently exempt from the Mormon edict against profanity. "Listen to me . . . Do you realize my family is at stake? Do you realize—excuse me, sir."

"So is mine," Massa volleyed.

"Excuse me for a second, sir," Beck continued. "My family is at stake. You've got a little scandal with your children in college. I've got one for all time now, because I'm not going to resign. I'm not going to back down. I have come to a place where I believe, at some point, the system will destroy me."

If anything's going to destroy Beck, it's his own mouth. But it's more mysterious to say it will be the "system." Which "they" operate.

Of course, just because you're paranoid doesn't mean "they" aren't out to get you. When a collection of liberal groups gained some traction in their effort to persuade advertisers to drop Beck because he called Obama a racist, Beck saw in it another conspiracy.

"Has someone decided that they must destroy my career and silence me because we've stumbled onto something?" he asked. "Has there ever been a case in American history, outside of the hard-core radical progressive Woodrow Wilson, where an American president and administration tried to destroy the livelihood of a private citizen with whom they disagree? Can't think of any."

Beck argued that this is "the same thing" as Nixon's

enemies list, and likened it to Nazis rounding up Jews, cit-
ing, as he often does, Martin Niemöller's description of
the Gestapo: "First, they came for the socialists . . ." Asked
Beck: "What is that poem? First they came for the Jews and
I stayed silent?"

There's "they" again. And Beck, German by ethnicity,
likes playing the Jew in this scenario. "There is going to
be a witch hunt—I believe, in this country, and possibly
around the world—for two groups," he informed his audience another day. "The first group, Jews—it happens every
time. Second group, I think, conservatives."

So if you believe "they" in the government are trying
to silence if not kill you, it would be quite understandable
to be upset about it. This is where Beck acknowledges he
does "have something in common" with Howard Beale, the
unstable anchorman from the 1976 film *Network* who tells
viewers the world is falling apart and urges them: "Get up
right now and go to the window. Open it, and stick your
head out, and yell, 'I'M AS MAD AS HELL, AND I'M NOT
GOING TO TAKE THIS ANYMORE!'"

"That's the way I feel," Beck told his Fox viewers. "I do
wonder every night why you are not out your window just
crying out and saying I'm mad as hell and I'm not going to
take it anymore!"

Beck finds it inexplicable that people might interpret
such actions as a sign of mental-health problems. "The

media seems to be painting a picture of anyone who is worried enough to prepare for the future as crazy. Call them crazy. I'm crazy. You're crazy. We're all crazy together," he went on. "People now—starting in the media—tell you, 'Oh, you can't trust that Glenn Beck, he's crazy,' or I have something to gain, or I'm just a Republican hack in disguise. The obvious insinuation is—if you're watching this television show every night—you're one of those three as well."

What a crazy thought.

Some would call Beck crazy for ranking, in his list called "Top Ten Bastards of All Time," Franklin Roosevelt and Tiger Woods as more evil than Pol Pot, and Keith Olbermann more evil than Hitler. But maybe that was just good marketing for his book *Arguing with Idiots*.

Some would call Beck crazy for having on his show an actor dressed up in Colonial garb and pretending he is Thomas Paine while reading the words of Beck himself. The Paine impersonator listed the economic stimulus legislation as the equivalent of Pearl Harbor and the World Trade Center attack. But maybe that was just good television.

Beck will frequently pepper his thoughts with a "maybe I'm crazy" disclaimer. "Maybe I'm crazy for going down this road," he said after suggesting that Obama was attempting to enslave teenagers. "Maybe I'm crazy, and people say I am," he said before suggesting that the federal government aimed to take over states. "I'm on the verge of moral collapse at any time," he said on CNN one night in 2006, discussing an evangelical minister's sex scandal.

The paranoia inevitably came to the attention of Comedy Central, where Jon Stewart did an extended imitation of Beck before the chalkboard.

"Believing there should be a minimum standard for how much lead can be in our paint might lead to the government having the right to sterilize and kill Jews," Stewart/Beck declared. "I'm not saying that might be the case—I'm saying that's the case!"

"Follow me, America!" Stewart shouted, impersonating the standard opening for Beck's show. "Why am I the only one saying it?" he continued. "Am I crazy, or . . ." Stewart trailed off. "Okay," he said.

Stewart, at the chalkboard, followed Beck's circles, which purported to link America with Europe, then Russia, then China. "It's so ingenious it almost doesn't make any sense whatsoever," Stewart/Beck said, then later summarized the Beck worldview: "If you subscribe to an idea, you also subscribe to that idea's ideology, and to every possible negative consequence that holding that ideology applies when you carry it to absurd extremes. For instance, progressives, if you believe in a minimal safety net for the nation's neediest, you believe in total and absolute government control."

Then Stewart turned the philosophy against its creator:

"If you believe that faith provides a strong moral template for our nation's foundation, it can only lead to totalitarian theocracy." With that, he drew more Beckian circles on the board and pasted up a photo of the Ayatollah Khomeini.

"That was hysterical," Beck reported on his show the next night about Stewart's parody. "He's saying that I'm crazy and all of this kind of stuff."

But Beck isn't crazy. Crazy is just part of his repertoire. If there was any doubt about this, it should have been dispelled way back in November 2006, when Beck took a call on his radio show accusing him of racism.

"Let me just, wait wait, Rod," he told the caller. "I'm not just going to let you throw down these race cards because obviously you're somebody who likes to throw the race card and you don't even understand what the race card is," Beck said calmly.

The caller also wasn't pleased with Beck's joke about wishing a nuclear explosion in France. "I stand by that," Beck said.

The caller began to retreat from his accusation—"all right, so if I'm wrong"—but Beck had plans for him.

"Oh, you know what? I'm not even going to tolerate this anymore, Rod. Because you, obviously, sir—" Beck began calmly. Then, suddenly, he erupted. "GET OFF MY PHONE!! . . . Do I want to vaporize France? AS MUCH AS I WANT TO VAPORIZE YOU!!" Beck was leaning forward in his chair, waving his arms madly and shrieking. "You're lucky I don't have some sort of equipment where I could vaporize you right now because I'd keep pushing the button over and over and over and over and over again!" Beck calmed momentarily, and said, "Now that, sir, is what I would call comedy. Do I really want to vaporize you?" Beck returned to his screaming: "YES I DO!!"

Beck flipped on his theme music, then leaned back in his chair. He was perfectly calm, and wearing an enormous grin. Still smiling, he took a swig from the bottle in front of him. The fury, the violent talk, the shouting—in short, the craziness? All for show.

CHAPTER 6
A HEMORRHOID ON THE BODY POLITIC

· ·

Countless people have considered Glenn Beck to be a pain in the ass. But for once, he was the one with a sore bottom.

"I'm just at home, and I'm recovering from some surgery that was scheduled and then went horribly awry," Beck, stubbly-faced, his head on a pillow, said to the camera for a video that was posted on his Web site. "I said on the way to the hospital, if I die, God forbid this makes it into the paper. I want to make sure this is not the way I'm remembered."

Understandably. Beck nearly met his end because of botched hemorrhoid surgery.

Just after Christmas 2007, he was admitted to a hospital for outpatient surgery on his rear end, but then woke up on the operating table. The painkillers were so intense they impaired his breathing. He went home, only to return a couple of hours later to the emergency room, where he found the service most unacceptable. He needed a catheter because he couldn't urinate, and wound up spending five days in the hospital in a narcotics-induced haze. He found the hospital staff—MSNBC viewers, perhaps—to be rude and generally unconcerned about his pain and suffering.

When he got home, he began to plan a multimedia assault on the American health-care system. "Don't talk to me about health care," he wrote on his Web site. "Don't talk to me about HMOs. Don't talk to me about anything else. Don't talk to me about how you need a new CAT scan. Don't talk to me about how you need a new facility. Talk to me about how you could have a hospital full of people that don't see people in pain."

He discussed the gory details: "Your bladder usually holds about 400 ccs. My bladder, when they finally emptied it, was 1,500." He spoke of hopelessness: "By Saturday night I was ready to kill myself."

Overall, he said in his video, "it was one of the most eye-opening experiences of my life to receive health care in the United States today in not one of our more glorious medical institutions, even though I live in a very nice area. This hospital . . . was phenomenal, phenomenally bad." Beck had no mercy for the capitalists running this cruel place. "I have some stories that will melt your brain. And hopefully will melt the brain of the CEO of this hospital, to wake him up to find out what's going on and it should be a wake-up call to all of us, because this is one of the hospitals where the president of GE is going. If they don't care about the president of GE, you really think they care about schlubs that are just average working stiffs?"

Beck sounded like a changed man. "I think it really opened my eyes," he told his followers. "Join me for my new perspective on life, our health-care system, and blood shooting from places blood should not shoot out of," he said, teasing his upcoming show.

Beck was still on CNN. In January 2008, he went back on the air and spoke of his "personal voyage through the nightmare that is our health-care system." He began the show by saying: "No matter how much the health-care system would try to keep me down, I'm back . . . Getting well in this country could actually almost kill you."

For those not paying attention, Beck filled them in. "It was butt surgery. I had surgery on my ass." He said he had seen the health-care system "at its very worst." He complained that he was "nothing more than a number," and "I felt like I was at a DMV." He acknowledged that "we do have a health-care crisis in this country," even if he didn't think the government or the insurance companies could fix it.

The next day, Beck was on *Good Morning America* with a similar message. "Let's emphasize the word 'care' in health care," he proposed.

Alas, it seems that this was the painkillers talking.

Within mere months, Beck had forgotten his complaints about the health-care system. In June 2008, he played a clip of Barack Obama campaigning for the White House with a promise for health-care reform: "We will be able to look back and tell our children that this was the moment when we began to provide care for the sick."

Retorted Beck: "America already has the best health care in the world. We do take care of our sick."

Never mind that "nightmare that is our health-care system." Beck now boasted that the United States was the place where "anybody who's sick and wealthy in the world" comes. "You're about to lose the best health-care system in the world," he told his viewers. He saw no reason to "spend $1 trillion to overhaul the best health-care system in the world."

"The best health-care system in the world and you're going to change it?" he demanded. "Republicans, call their bluff!"

As it happens, Beck was about to have another experience inside the best health-care system in the world. He was doing his daily radio broadcast one day in November 2009 when he began to complain on air that he wasn't feeling well. He left the show and went to a Manhattan hospital, where he underwent surgery for appendicitis. There were no complications this time—outside of *The Daily Show*, that is, on which Stewart gave Beck a taste of his own medicine.

"This appendix thing is not an isolated incident!" the comedian said, adding that "the stakes are nothing less than Glenn Beck's internal organs!"

After some Beckian weeping, Stewart went on: "I'm just a concerned American citizen like you questioning what's going on inside Glenn Beck, and if you don't get these answers, you ask again and again and again! Because you know who else didn't answer medical questions? Hitler."

And that was before the conspiracy against Glenn Beck's health claimed another victim: his eyesight. In July 2010 he told followers that he had an eye condition called macular dystropy, and "could go blind in the next year."

It was tricky to parody Beck, because Stewart could come up with nothing more outlandish than things Beck himself had said in earnest. He had, for example, presented an extended comparison between Obama's health-care plan and Nazi efforts to build a master race.

It began even before the health-care push. "So here you have Barack Obama going in and spending money on embryonic stem cell research," he said after Obama lifted the ban on such federal research. "Remember, those great progressive doctors are the ones who brought us eugenics . . . In case you don't know what eugenics led us to: the Final Solution. A master race! A perfect person . . . The stuff that we are facing is absolutely frightening. So I guess I have to put my name on yes, I hope Barack Obama fails."

It was a slippery-slope argument greased with Crisco. "When we put science in front of ethics," Beck reasoned, "we start having a bunch of people walking around, especially progressive scientists, walking around in little white coats and talking about—hey, we can make the master race?"

When Democrats began to float their health-care proposals, there was no mention of eugenics, but Beck was not fooled. "What does this new health-care system that they're trying to push through in the middle of the night have to do with eugenics? The seed, the germ," he explained.

The seed was planted. Beck cultivated it regularly. In August 2009, as lawmakers' "town-hall" meetings were exploding in anger over health-care reform, Beck gave the demonstrators plenty to be angry about.

"You have three people in the White House that are in love with eugenics or whatever it is you would call it today," Beck informed his radio listeners. "Please, dear God, read history. Please, dear God, read the truth of what these people have said in their own words, and ask yourself this one question: Do you trust these people enough to give them control over who lives and who dies?"

A few nights later, Beck was detailing the supposedly pro-eugenics views. One of the guilty was the head of regulatory policy, Cass Sunstein. His offense? "One of his good friends," an academic named Peter Singer, wrote an article titled "Why We Must Ration Health Care." Never mind that Sunstein himself hadn't said any such thing: Guilt by association was evidence enough in Beck's court.

Beck turned to his guests, author R. J. Pestritto, law professor Carter Snead, and former Bush administration official John Hoff. "Gentlemen, first of all, does anybody here believe eugenics is coming, building a master race?"

His guests did not believe this. "No, sir, absolutely not," came the reply. It was time for Beck to find some new guests. Sure enough, he was back a few weeks later with Pastor Stephen Broden, who claimed to have chronicled "the eugenics movement and black genocide taking place in America today."

Beck genuinely seemed to be convinced that an African American president, advised by a Jewish chief of staff, was intent on building a master race. "The reason why I bring up Hitler so much of the time is because what he did, many of the things, had their roots, their seeds here in America," Beck explained. "The progressive tactics haven't changed much since then."

Beck's tactics hadn't changed much either. His own displeasure with the health-care system was now a distant memory. He set about demonstrating that Obama's health-care legislation would cause rationing of care and euthanasia of the old and infirm. "Really, this is the beginning," he argued. "I mean, you know, the extreme example is what happened in Germany . . . Sometimes for the common good, you just have to say, 'Hey Grandpa, you've had a good life. Sucks to be you.'"

There was nothing in the proposed bill that even hinted at such an idea, but Beck offered proof in the form of constant repetition. "The government is going to have to start rationing care during the last six months of life," he said with certainty. "There's going to be waiting lines and there's going to be some bureaucrat deciding whether or not you should die."

When Sarah Palin came out with her "death panel" allegation in August 2009—adding fuel to that month's town-hall conflagration, Beck quickly endorsed the theme. "That's quite a statement. I believe it to be true," he said of the accusation that the law would create euthanasia boards. After Obama himself pointed out that there was no such thing in the proposal, Beck came back with this: "He was saying yesterday in this meeting that nobody's going to snuff out your grandma, and the crowd was laughing. You laugh all the way to the death panels."

Beck continued to defend Palin's death-panels accusation. "She is right," he proclaimed. "Basically, they come up with the number of maximum treatment costs per year to keep you alive." Again, there was nothing about this in the bill.

As the health-care bill followed its tortuous route to passage, Beck kept up the barrage: "Somebody is not going to get a kidney transplant. Somebody is not going to get heart surgery. Somebody is not going to get chemotherapy." Specifically, Beck forecast that by age forty, "you're starting to outlive your usefulness," and by seventy, "you're out of luck, Jack."

Whenever a new allegation bubbled up through the conservative blogosphere, Beck took it to his viewers. There was, for example, the accusation, based on nothing but imagination, that those who don't heed the "individual mandate" to have health insurance will be locked away in prison. "If you don't play ball with them now, if you don't get into their government health care, there will be jail time." (In reality, the legislation expressly forbids imprisoning those who refuse.)

Another day, Beck spun an entire fantasy about what health-care legislation would do—including dietary restrictions and deciding who can reproduce. "They will tell you what to eat," he intoned. "If you can be deemed someone who maybe shouldn't have a baby, they can have their people come in. The government is in our homes on this."

The health-care debate went painfully on and on, like a botched hemorrhoid operation. At each stage, Beck found a new way to describe the bill as the End of the World as We Know It.

"Your freedom is at stake. This is the moment. This is the bill. You must not allow this to pass," he said in November 2009. "It will be a nail in the coffin of America . . . You must wake everybody up you know. This is the end of prosperity in America forever if this bill passes. This is the end of America as you know it."

In January, he declared that Democrats were declaring "the government God, our creator." He added: "This is the end of the American Constitution."

The next month, he summoned his troops to the ramparts. "Republicans, you filibuster! You do everything you can!" he said. If the bill passes, "the Republic has frayed beyond, possibly, beyond repair." He spoke of revenge at the polls, "assuming there's a country left for a next election."

In March, he escalated to visions of violence. "If it passes," Beck said, Obama will have "the pieces that the president needs to control every aspect of your life, to fundamentally transform America." And if it doesn't pass, "those on the left are going to become violent." The laws will, he said, "rip this country in half."

Yet the bill continued its halting progress toward eventual passage. Dr. Beck took out an X-ray film on the set. "What they're about to pass is not a tumor," he said. "What they're about to pass is a bloodstream disease. It will be injected into our system and it will be incurable . . . The fundamental transformation of America is here."

The bill passed. And, as of this writing, there are still no death panels, no eugenics, no euthanasia, nobody being sent to prison, no ripping in half of the country, no end of America as we know it, no nail in America's coffin. Then again, maybe this is because of the painkillers; any day now, we could wake up with a huge pain in our national butt.

CHAPTER 7
THE MIDAS TOUCH

. . . .

Let us now hear from Glenn Beck, regular guy.

"I am no different than you," he tells viewers, with genuine regular-guy grammar. "I am just a regular schmo that finds myself on a set in New York."

"Look, I'm a schmo," he confesses to a guest one night. "I really don't know how all this stuff works."

"By the end of World War I, the power had shifted," he informs his audience another night, "and really the schlubs—people like you and me, we didn't even know it."

"Back before the Enlightenment," he says on still another occasion, "there were kings and rulers, lords and ladies, the landowners, and then there were the serfs, everybody else, people like you and me."

A Tea Party leader is described as a "regular schmo just like you and me." Beck says the government has a dim view of "dummies like you and me." He asks whether the chairman of the House Ways and Means Committee is "part of the ruling class or is he with you and me." He says that "if it were up to you or me, just regular schmoes in America, the Freedom Tower would have been done years ago."

Since Beck is using Yiddish when he speaks of schmoes and of schlubs, let's do the same: It takes chutzpah to carry on with this shtick.

When he finishes his regular-guy routine at Fox studios in Manhattan, Beck hops into his chauffer-driven sedan and takes the drive home to New Canaan, Connecticut, ranked by CNN Money in 2008 as the place with the highest median family income in the nation. The man who has just described himself as a "serf" rather than a "landowner" disembarks and steps into his sixteen-room neo-Colonial mansion on Ponus Ridge (Ponus was the Greek god of hard labor), which he purchased in 2005 for $4.25 million. Perhaps he winds down by taking a swim in the pool or strolling his 2.87 acres bordering Laurel Reservoir. When Beck, on the air, claims he lives in a "subdivision," his followers probably don't picture the compound on Ponus Ridge. It is a castle fit for a king, but unlike other castles, Beck's, sadly, did not come with fortifications. So he built them. He showed up at the New Canaan Zoning Commission office in 2008 with his wife and his bodyguard and his lawyer, demanding an exemption from zoning laws to allow him to surround himself on all sides with a six-foot barrier: a four-foot stone wall topped by two feet of wood fencing in the front, and a six-foot wooden barrier elsewhere.

The lawyer explained to the town elders how a portion of the wall had "already mistakenly been built." Oops! A neighbor and board members said they didn't think fortifying the Beck estate was necessary. The *New Canaan Advertiser* wrote that at the meeting, Beck's lawyer explained that Beck was a hunted man. The barrier "won't stop them but it will slow them down," the attorney said. "It will stop anything people send into the property, whether photographs or bullets."

Bullets! On Ponus Ridge in New Canaan! It was sounding like one of those postapocalyptic scenarios on Beck's show, when people defend their property with guns and plant vegetables to survive. In reality, the closest the New Canaan police came to witnessing that sort of violence was "a report" about "an individual banging on a door" at Beck's manse.

The commoner/serf/schmo Beck describes his business empire as if he's running a convenience store. "I'm a small businessman," he explains. "I do radio, I do television and Internet. I write books. I print a news and humor magazine. And I built it all from scratch with the help of an amazing group of people."

His is a rags-to-nicer-rags tale. Or perhaps he would

use the Yiddish word for rags, *schmattas*. "In 1999, only in America—in 1999, I couldn't afford my rent of $695 a month," he says. "Things have changed, and as of right now, my business is doing pretty well. But just like you, I'm concerned about tomorrow."

But not that concerned. His business empire, according to *Forbes*, is worth $32 million a year: $13 million in publishing from his books (he has a profit-sharing deal with Simon & Schuster) and his *Fusion* magazine; $10 million for radio (actually $450 million over five years); $4 million from his Web site; $3 million from tours and speaking (he does comedy shows in addition to the Bold & Fresh Tour with Bill O'Reilly); and a mere $2 million from Fox News to round out the portfolio.

Beck does not let the schlubs and schmoes in his audience know about such riches, but he was happy to boast about them to the elites. He allowed a *Forbes* reporter to follow him around for "several days" to report a story on his empire. The reporter found such regular-guy staples in Beck's life as the cockatoo he rented for $750 a night as a prop for his stage performance.

Beck, the magazine reported, has thirty-four full-time staffers (that apparently doesn't include the staff of similar size provided for him by Fox). He has a publicist separate from Fox and travels everywhere with bodyguards. His media empire (it has changed its name from Mercury

Radio Arts to Glenn Beck Inc.) nearly rivals Oprah's in its clout. In May 2010, Beck boasted that five of the titles in the Amazon top twenty-five bestseller list were books he had promoted on air: *George Washington's Sacred Fire* (number 1), *The Real George Washington* (8), *Samuel Adams: A Life* (15), Beck's yet-to-be-published *The Overton Window* (16), and *The 5,000 Year Leap* (22).

When Beck does describe his huge income, he does so with a "spread the wealth" philosophy that sounds a lot like the Barack Obama view that Joe the Plumber condemned. "I think it's obscene to have that kind of earning potential and not spread the wealth with the people who help you to get there," Beck writes. He also says he tithes 10 percent of his earnings. "Once you commit to giving away your 10 percent, you will get so much more," he said.

Of course, when you make what Beck does, it is probably less painful to give away 10 percent than it is for the typical working schlub with whom Beck identifies. Beck's own prescriptions for America would cause his millions to be taxed much less while increasing taxes on the schmoes and schlubs. He proposes a federal flat tax on income and mentions no exemption for the poor or middle class: "Reduce the size of government in half," he proposed on his Fox show in 2010. "Flat tax of 12 to 15 percent." Because most of Beck's income should be in the 35 percent tax bracket, this would reduce his own payments by nearly two-thirds. The nearly half of all Americans who pay no federal income taxes—the schlubs and schmoes, as Beck might say—would see their tax obligations rise sharply.

Beck originally named his business after Orson Welles's Mercury Theatre radio series. He writes in his 2003 book, *The Real America*, that he admires the way Welles figured out that he could be more efficient if he had an ambulance take him from job to job. He wasn't sick, but it saved time: "Welles hired an ambulance to pick him up from the Broadway show, turn the sirens on, and take him to CBS, where he played a role on the radio," Beck writes. "Then they would pack him back in the ambulance, turn the sirens on again and go back to the Broadway theater to do the second show."

Some might regard this as fraud; Beck regards it as pure genius. "Welles inspired me to believe that I can create anything that I can see or imagine," he concludes. Even if it is based on a lie.

To the chagrin of Fox News, Beck, even as he has chased away advertisers, has done an exceptional job marketing one product: himself. He often directs Fox viewers to his own Web site, GlennBeck.com, encouraging them to purchase an elite membership. One night, he devoted a segment to promoting his own one-man show on Broadway.

"Tomorrow night here in New York at the Nokia Theater in Times Square I'm doing a program," Beck told Fox viewers. "You can see it on 'The Insider' at GlennBeck .com." That's the pay-extra membership class. "I'm doing a show called 'The Future of History' because we've got to learn history to be able to face our future."

What brings all of Beck's moneymaking ventures—TV, radio, Web, publishing, speaking—together is a common theory that doomsday means payday. Though it's a huge audience for cable news, Beck's viewership as a proportion of the American public is small: 0.9 percent. Though figures are less reliable for radio, that audience could be as high as 3 percent of the population.

But this tiny slice of the American public is passionate and highly motivated, and they will evidently do, and buy, what Glenn Beck tells them to do and buy. If he tells them that the world economy is collapsing, that currencies are becoming worthless, and that they should buy gold, they buy gold. Conveniently enough, a top sponsor of Beck's radio, TV, and Internet ventures is Goldline, a big gold dealer.

Go to GlennBeck.com and you see a banner advertisement across the top: "Goldline. Trusted and Used by Glenn Beck." To the right of that is another ad, with a photo of Beck: "Goldline International. Get Your Free Investor Kit." Below that is a third ad: "Click for a free investment kit. Trusted and used by Glenn Beck." His smiling face is next to a gold coin. If you click on the ads, you'll wind up at a site announcing "Glenn Beck Recommends Goldine" or a photo of Beck and his testimonial: "Before I started turning you on to Goldline, I wanted to look them in the eye. This is a top-notch organization that's been in business since 1960." Other links say, "Goldline Is Glenn Beck's Choice for Gold" and give the advice that "some analysts believe that gold may rise to several thousand dollars per ounce."

Among those "analysts" is Beck himself. He has the Goldline president, Mark Albarian, on his show frequently, interviewing his sponsor about the merits of gold. "So, Mark, I saw a story last night that said we're . . . we're running out of gold," Beck began one such interview. "Is that even possible?"

"I think it is," Albarian replied. "Now, we won't actually run out of gold, but you'll see much higher prices in my opinion."

Beck said a price of $2,500 per ounce would be "reasonable." It was about $1,100 an ounce at the time of the interview.

"There was an article on AOL where they talked about how you could get to $2,750," Albarian added.

"I think people are running out of options on what, you know, could be worth something at all," Beck said. "You have to think like a German Jew, 1934." Extending the analogy to Weimar hyperinflation, Beck predicted that people could "make more in the commodities in the short term than they can in the dollar because the dollar is going to continue to fall."

Seven months after this forecast, gold had climbed 9 percent—not bad. But the dollar, which Beck predicted would collapse, was up more than twice as much over that same period—21 percent against the euro.

But for Beck, it's always a good time to buy gold, particularly from Goldline. Back in December 2008, he had Albarian on his show and the host spoke of a "1989-style Soviet collapse" for the American economy. "Still a good time to buy gold?" he asked.

"It's always a good time," said the gold dealer.

That message is a constant theme of Beck's "the end is near" broadcasts. Sometimes on his chalkboard he will scribble "God, gold, guns"—the three safe harbors in a societal collapse.

One night he held up a gold coin and explained how the dollar's value will fall to the point where "we no longer can afford energy. We no longer can afford clothing. We can no longer afford bread or anything else." One other evening, Beck's guest, "trend forecaster" Gerald Celente, announced that gold "topped over $1,000 an ounce today . . . By 2015, you're going to see gold probably at $8,000 an ounce."

Another time, Beck was delighted to announce that "in the time that I was on the air, gold shot up $50." He boasted in one interview with O'Reilly that gold was "significantly over $1,000 an ounce."

"That's because of you," O'Reilly joked. "You're selling it every two minutes on your radio show."

That he is, and on his TV show, too. "The smart money is saying, 'Hunker down, things could get much worse,'" was his investment counsel one night. On the radio, he told an anxious caller named Debbie that "it is increasingly possible that hyperinflation is coming our way," so "we need to hedge our bet against that." He went on to say that "gold has always been that doorframe" in an earthquake. "Doorframes are the safest place because it's reinforced . . . Look at gold as the threshold, as a doorframe."

In one of his paid plugs for Goldline on the radio, Beck began with a joking preface—"Don't tell anyone I'm getting paid for this commercial"—before recommending the purchase of gold "as an insurance policy" against calamity. "I hope I'm wrong in all the things that might be coming our way," but "God only knows what tomorrow will bring," he warned. "Check out Goldline," he suggested. "Pray on it, make sure it's right for you."

When the *New York Times* inquired about such paid sponsorship (Goldline listed Beck as a "paid spokesman" on its Web site), Fox News said it had sought "clarification" from Beck about his work for Goldline and was assured that "he is not a paid spokesman." That's a relief, because Fox policy "prohibits any on-air talent from endorsing products or serving as a product spokesperson."

It's also a good thing that Beck taped his promotional

video for Goldline before he arrived at Fox. He talked about how the Founding Fathers—a favorite topic on his broadcasts—believed the country was "going to shake apart and there would be troubled times" before it recovered. "I'd like a little bit of insurance. That's why I want to talk to you about Goldline," Beck explained over soft music. "If you're like our Founding Fathers, Thomas Jefferson and John Adams, then just know that what's on the horizon is just temporary and this too shall pass. Here's the deal. Call Goldline." He added later, "You want some insurance? Trust the people at Goldline."

Beck's constant pitching for Goldline came to the attention of his ideological critics, one of whom, Democratic congressman Anthony Weiner of New York, issued a "report" condemning the gold dealer's practices: "Goldline Grossly Overcharges for Their Coins"; "Goldline Falsely Claims to Offer 'Good' Investments'"; "Goldline Salespeople Misrepresent Their Ability to Give 'Investment Advice'"; and "Goldline Formed an Unholy Alliance with Conservative Pundits to Drive a False Narrative."

Beck responded by creating a new Web site, WeinerFacts .com, showing the congressman's head on a walking hot dog. He went on O'Reilly's show to respond to Weiner by eating a wiener. O'Reilly said the congressman "is accusing you of being Goldfinger."

"A lot of wieners do that," Beck said. He went on to

argue that Goldline has an "A-plus credit rating from the Better Business Bureau."

There's some dispute about Goldline's ratings and reputation, but that's hardly the important point. The problem is not that Beck sends people to a shoddy company. It's that he frightens his audience into thinking they need to buy gold because an economic Armageddon is approaching—and then they go and buy gold from a company that pays Beck in hard currency.

The regular schmo may not be aware that fellow schmo Beck has such expensive tastes. And the ordinary schlub probably doesn't know fellow schlub Beck is making a lot of money by scaring him into buying gold.

Advertisers, however, are a bit savvier. And some of the most common brand names in America have fled Beck's show in a panic—not because they fear an apocalypse, but because they fear the host's mouth.

The trouble began in the summer of 2009 when Beck determined that President Obama had a "deep-seated hatred for white people or the white culture." A little-known African American group called Color of Change launched a boycott, and several big advertisers—Walmart, GMAC, Best Buy, CVS, Travelocity, Geico, ConAgra, RadioShack, State Farm, and Procter & Gamble—fell into line.

At first, other advertisers took their place, and Beck supporters pushed back on a Web site called DefendGlenn

.com. Color of Change claimed it had Fox revenue figures showing a sharp drop for the show, but Fox maintained that it hadn't lost money because the advertisers merely switched to other Fox shows.

But then Fox's Carl Cameron reported that Color of Change had been cofounded by White House environmental adviser Van Jones. By coincidence or design, Jones became the focus of a daily attack on Beck's show. The "self-avowed communist" Jones, with a history of questionable rhetoric that Beck exposed, was pressured within a couple of weeks to quit his White House job.

Just as the boycott over the "racist" accusation was quieting down, Beck found himself in a new dispute with liberal church leaders. As part of his war against "progressives," Beck told his followers that they should quit their churches if there was any mention of "social justice" or "economic justice" in those houses of worship. "I beg you, look for the words social justice or economic justice on your church Web site. If you find them, run as fast as you can. Social justice and economic justice, they are code words," Beck advised. "Am I advising people to leave their church? Yes . . . If you have a priest that is pushing social justice, go find another parish."

In the usual style, Beck embroidered the case against "social justice" and "economic justice" churches with accusations of "socialism, Marxism, communism," and pronounced that these churchgoing progressives "are not a friend of Jesus Christ." Of the social justice types in churches, Beck alleged: "The enemy is within our gates." Calling them "the same people that tried to destroy Christmas," he said they aim to get into a church and "rot it from the inside."

This war on social justice was startling to many churchgoers and church officials alike, who had often been using the term for such activities as soup kitchens and medical clinics—not exactly evidence that the churches are rotting from the inside and harboring enemies. Other instances in which this nefarious "social justice" has been invoked through the years have included opposition to slavery and segregation.

The Reverend Jim Wallis, a liberal evangelical, called for another Beck boycott. "When your political philosophy is to consistently favor the rich over the poor, you don't want to hear about economic justice," Wallis said of Beck.

Beck, on the air, suggested that the Obama White House was behind the boycotts—a tricky claim to make because Jones had left Color for Change long before the boycott was called and Wallis was not, as Beck alleged, Obama's "spiritual and political adviser."

By the spring of 2010, *Washington Post* media critic Howard Kurtz reported that more than two hundred companies had joined the Beck boycott. A few, including Apple, had left Fox entirely. Those at the network acknowledged that they could charge more for advertising if the host wasn't so radioactive—but, then again, if the host wasn't so radioactive, the show wouldn't have so many passionate followers.

Though it was small consolation, Fox was able to find some less august advertisers, such as Goldline, to fill the spots vacated by the big brands. Another of the brands that came to Beck's rescue was Kaopectate.

CHAPTER 8
GLENN BECK'S LOVE AFFAIR
WITH HITLER

After the Obama administration bailed out General Motors and Chrysler, Glenn Beck invited onto his radio show a couple who lost their car dealership as part of the restructuring. Beck's thoughts went where they often go: to Nazi Germany.

"This is fascism!" he screamed. "This is what happens when you merge special interests, corporations, and the government. This is what happens. And you know what, guys; if people like you don't take a stand and I'm not suggesting that you don't sign or do sign . . . but at some point, you know what poem keeps going through my mind is 'First They Came for the Jews.' People, all of us, are like, well, this news doesn't really affect me. Well, I'm not a bondholder. Well, I'm not in the banking industry. Well, I'm not a big CEO. Well, I'm not on Wall Street. Well, I'm not a car dealer. I'm not an autoworker. Gang, at some point they're going to come for you!"

This was a rather unusual rendition of Martin Niemöller's famous lines about the Holocaust ("First, they came for the socialists . . ."), but for Beck, it was standard operating procedure. A few months later, he again invoked the Niemöller passage on his radio show, but this time he and his colleagues at Fox News were the Jewish victims being rounded up for extermination. The Gestapo in this case was the Obama White House, which was denying Fox's interview requests because of its hostile coverage of Obama.

He recommended journalists at other news outlets keep in mind "the old 'First they came for the Jews and I wasn't Jewish.' When you have a question and you believe that something should be asked, they're totally fine with you right now," Beck said. "When they're done with Fox and talk radio, do you really think they're going to leave you alone if you want to ask a tough question? If you believe that, you should open up a history book because you missed the point of many brutal dictators. You missed the point on how they always start."

For much of the last seventy years, there has been an unwritten rule followed by both sides in the American political debate: Try to avoid the Hitler accusations. Once you compare your opponent to the Nazis, any form of rational discussion becomes impossible; opponents take offense, and an apology usually follows. Richard Durbin, the number two Democrat in the Senate, gave a tearful apology for likening U.S. treatment of detainees to the Nazis, while Republican former House speaker Newt Gingrich climbed down from his claim that Obama is as·much of a threat to America as Adolf Hitler.

But Beck, it would seem, has a Nazi fetish. In his first fourteen months on Fox News, he and his guests invoked Hitler 115 times. Nazis, another 134 times. Fascism, 172 times. The Holocaust got 58 mentions, and Joseph Goebbels got 8 mentions.

Whenever Beck is talking about the president, the risk of a Nazi comparison is high. In September 2009, he was playing an old tape of Obama saying he favors a "single-payer" government-run health-care system. "I am not comparing him to this, but read *Mein Kampf* for this reason," Beck told his radio listeners. "You see that Hitler told you what he was going to do. He told the Germans." Not that he's comparing Obama to this, naturally.

Beck has been on the Nazi beat for some time. Back in 2006, he saw Nazism in Al Gore's book *An Inconvenient Truth*: "It's like Hitler. Hitler said a little bit of truth, and then he mixed in 'and it's the Jews' fault.' That's where things get a little troublesome, and that's exactly what's happening."

Exactly. That went so well that a year later, he likened Gore's global warming campaign to the Holocaust:

> Now, I'm not saying that anybody's going to—you know Al Gore's not going to be rounding up Jews and exterminating them. It is the same tactic, however. The goal is different. The goal is globalization. The goal is global carbon tax. The goal is the United Nations running the world. That is the goal. Back in the 1930s, the goal was get rid of all of the Jews and have one global government.

The comparison continued as Beck likened the work of global warming scientists to Hitler's eugenics and building a master race. "You got to have an enemy to fight," he said. "And when you have an enemy to fight, then you can unite the entire world behind you, and you seize power. That was Hitler's plan. His enemy: the Jew. Al Gore's enemy, the U.N.'s enemy: global warming . . . And you must silence all dissenting voices. That's what Hitler did."

The Anti-Defamation League pleaded with Beck to stop. "Glenn Beck's linkage of Hitler's plan to round up and exterminate Jews with Al Gore's efforts to raise awareness of global warming is outrageous, insensitive, and deeply offensive," Abe Foxman said at the time.

But Beck only expanded his fascist fantasies when he moved to Fox News and Obama came to power. In April

2009, he dedicated entire shows to the subject. "The government is crushing our freedom under steel-toe boots," he began one such show. "Americans on both sides are now saying, 'You know, haven't I seen this movie before?'" As he said these words, the screen on the set with him showed Nazis marching. "Enough!" Beck shouted, proposing that the "tea parties" and the "9/12 Project," which he created, oppose the fascists.

"People once again are feeling oppressed by an out-of-control state," he said, furthering the Obama–Hitler analogy. "They're going to nationalize our banks, they're going to put the government in charge of private payrolls, they're going to move to nationalize our auto industry. And here's the one key word—using the word 'crisis' to obtain the unprecedented power needed to make it all happen."

Beck, deciding belatedly that the Bush administration, too, had fascist tendencies, continued: "It all adds up to me now having to admit that I was wrong. Our government is not marching down the road towards communism or socialism . . . They're marching us to a brand of nonviolent fascism, or to put it another way, they're marching us towards 1984—'Big Brother,' he's watching."

"Like it or not, fascism is on the rise," Beck announced, softening this only a touch by saying, "It's fascism with a happy face. To those who said fascism is coming under Bush and the people who are saying fascism is coming under Obama: You're both right!"

Beck brought out his Obama-as-fascist expert. "Fascism sought to control indirectly through the domination of nominally private owners. Would you say that this is what's happening with GM right now, and AIG?" American companies, Beck said, are behaving as German companies did in "the early days of Adolf Hitler."

When his guest, libertarian writer Sheldon Richman, tried to offer some cautions, Beck took umbrage. "I am not saying that Barack Obama is a fascist," he argued, having just outlined a case making that very point. "I'm not saying the Democrats are fascists. I'm saying the government under Bush and under Obama and under all of the presidents that we've seen or at least most of the presidents that we've seen for quite some time are slowly but surely moving us away from our republic and into a system of fascism."

He just didn't get that upset about it when Bush was in office. "Like it or not, fascism is on the rise," he warned. "The government is a heroin pusher, using smiley-faced fascism to grow the nanny state." American progressives, he said at another point, "had a love affair" with Mussolini.

Beck drew a direct link between how "Hitler used the world economic crisis as a pivot point" and the words of Obama's (Jewish) chief of staff Rahm Emanuel: "You never want a serious crisis to go to waste."

Beck, with the help of his guests, determined that "there are a lot of similarities" between the current environment and the fall of Weimar Germany. Warning of German-style hyperinflation, he said: "We all know the world is on fire." He showed images of Hitler, Stalin, and Lenin and asked, "Is this where we're headed?"

"I'm not predicting that we go down that road," Beck said, after doing just that. "What I'm talking tonight about is: Destined to Repeat Fascism," he explained, giving the episode a name. "Whether it's the temperature in your house, because it's not good for the planet, all the way to, 'Well, I'm sorry, you've got to go to a camp.'" Beck was destined to repeat his fascist accusations, over and over. Touting a book titled *Lenin, Stalin and Hitler* on one show, he asserted: "It's all happening again. I'm not saying that these people are in our horizon, but let me tell you something: it's spooky, the similarities."

He's not saying, he's just saying.

Health-care reform, naturally, provided more Nazi linkages. When Walmart joined the fight, Beck commented: "It's what happened in the national socialist country of Germany in the 1930s under Hitler. These companies get into bed and think, 'Well, we're going to be fine. We'll take just a little bit of this.' Then they're trapped."

When Obama's advisers made a video to boost support for the reform, Beck saw a Nazi precedent. "Now remember, Goebbels, king of propaganda?" he asked. "This is yet another playbook, page taken right out of the playbook."

At another point, Beck told his viewers that "when I finish this story, some may believe we're on the road to the Hitler Youth." The source of this? A speech by Gore, to children and teens at a youth conference. Recalling that some in his parents' generation could no longer defend racial segregation, Gore said: "That's when the laws started to change. There are some things about our world that you know that older people don't know."

From this, Beck concluded: "The government and its friends are indoctrinating our children for control of their minds, your freedom, and our choice and our future. It must stop, because history—when properly taught—has already shown us where it leads. This is what Nazi Joseph Goebbels said about the Hitler Youth: 'If such an art of active mass influence through propaganda is joined with a long-term systematic education of our nation and if both are conducted in a unified and precise way, the relationship between the leadership and the nation will always remain close.'"

Beck also found fascism in Obama's 2008 campaign speech calling for an expansion of the Peace Corps, Ameri-Corps, and the Foreign Service. "We cannot continue to rely only on our military in order to achieve the national security objectives that we've set," he argued. "We've got to have a civilian national security force that's just as powerful, just as strong, just as well-funded."

"This is what Hitler did with the SS," Beck told one

of his guests. "He had his own people. He had the brown shirts and then the SS. This is what Saddam Hussein . . . I mean, I think America would have a really hard time getting their arms around that."

Moments later, Beck added, "I'm not suggesting anything. I'm asking questions. I don't know what this means."

But—what the heck?—why not trot out an SS comparison anyway?

Beck used the occasion of a shooting at the national Holocaust Museum to share his view that "the Germans" during Hitler's rise "were an awful lot like we are now. We're kind of living in a denial, like, no, that can't really be happening.

"All right. The climate change people are pulling a page from Nazis' Hitler youth."

Beck brought in the conservative writer Jonah Goldberg, for reinforcement. "What a nightmare this is!" Beck told him. "Can you give me any example in history where this kind of stuff has happened, what's happening today, and what does it lead to?"

Goldberg could. "I'm not calling Barack Obama a Hitler and I'm not calling him Nazis and all the rest," he began. Right, it always starts this way. "But you know, in fascism, we saw the people's car. We call it the Volkswagen . . . Now we've got Barack Obama saying that G.M. is going to make these affordable fuel-efficient cars."

Silly, perhaps, but there was something deft about the constant Obama-as-Nazi allegations. In most cases where anybody hurls "fascist" allegations, it's usually the left hurling them at the right. Conservatives, meanwhile, hurl the "communist" charge at the left. But Beck found a way around this paradigm. Progressives, he figured, are responsible for both fascism *and* communism. Conservatives, by contrast, are the opponents of both.

"The reason why I bring up Hitler so much," he told his Nazism-saturated viewers one night, "is because what he did—many of the things had their roots, their seeds here in America. The biggest example is eugenics, which led to extermination camps. This was a progressive idea . . . The Nazi eugenic idea evolved naturally into the eventual Holocaust and the deaths of six million Jews."

Goldberg was back as a guest, to explain that Hitler's "social agenda was for expanding universal access to health care, for expanding access to education. It was for [a] cradle to grave welfare state." That, and making lamp shades from human skin.

"Fascism and communism are the same," Beck deduced. In fact, "sometimes, it's hard to tell Hitler and Marx apart."

Particularly because, as far as Beck's viewers can tell, they both now live in the White House.

CHAPTER 9
WOODROW WILSON, SPAWN OF SATAN

* *

Just listen to the words Glenn Beck has been directing at the president:

"This is an evil SOB, man."

"One evil SOB—bad dude!"

"I mean, he's a dirtbag racist, is he not?"

"I hate this guy. I don't even want to show his picture. No, don't do it. Don't show it. I hate this guy."

"The biggest racist president [who] ever served."

"He was a horror show, wasn't he? A horror show, possibly the spookiest president we've ever had."

This is the sort of thing that might make the Secret Service worried about their protectee. But in this case, they can stand down: The president Beck is talking about died eighty-six years ago.

Beck's peculiar obsession with Woodrow Wilson is of

recent origin. "I mean, I got to tell you, two years ago, I knew nothing about Woodrow Wilson," he told his viewers. That, evidently, remains the case.

But Beck did read a conservative historian's book about the twenty-eighth president, and the Fox News host decided to blame Wilson for just about everything bad in the world today—including Barack Obama, born thirty-seven years after Wilson died.

Beck advertised this theme on his very first show on Fox, promising to tell viewers "what tactic Obama [is] borrowing from Woodrow Wilson" and that other ne'er-do-well, FDR, "to make sure his agenda gets pushed right straight through."

As promised, Beck was on the next night, venting his full fury at poor Woodrow. "A president I never really learned about in school at all, Woodrow Wilson—what an SOB this guy was!" he began.

Had he paid attention in school, Beck would have learned that Wilson was a conservative (!) political science professor and president of Princeton before he became New Jersey governor and then president in 1912. This was the "Progressive Era" in America, a period from about 1891 to 1921, and Wilson, like figures in both political parties in those days, ran on a progressive platform.

And that is why Beck hates him.

The Progressive Era was the time of muckrakers and

such things as the struggle to abolish child labor, break up monopolies, clean up meat-processing plants, and give women the right to vote. For Beck, this was a very dark time in our nation's history.

The Progressive Era may have ended ninety years ago, but for Beck it still haunts. "As I study history," the erudite host proclaims, "I see that a lot of the problems—most of the problems, in fact—stem from Woodrow Wilson and the progressive movement." Progressivism, he says, is "the cancer," the movement behind both Nazism and communism, a creed under which "people are secondary to the Earth and animals," a group of people who are "full-fledged eugenic racists," barbarians who "will cheat. They will lie. They will steal. And they have, in the past, blown things up if it helps them to win."

Those who call themselves "progressives" today have little in common with the Progressive Era of a century ago; it's largely a term liberals adopted for themselves after Republicans turned the word "liberal" into an epithet during the 1980s. Beck, however, was determined to draw a straight line from capital-P Progressives to modern-day progressives—a labor he undertook with great dedication from the moment of his arrival at Fox.

"Woodrow Wilson took Uncle Sam and that cartoon and tried to get America to cozy up to government power," he told his viewers on January 30, 2009. Realizing some might view this hundred-year-old history lesson as a little nutty, he added: "Are you regretting your decision to watch this show yet because all of a sudden, you're like, 'Why is he talking about Woodrow Wilson?' Hang on, I got a point here."

His point: Woodrow Wilson tried to make Uncle Sam look "kind of like Bernie Madoff, okay?"

Okay, Glenn.

Two weeks later, Beck was back, reporting that he had read more about the twenty-eighth president over the weekend. His conclusion remained: "Woodrow Wilson was a nightmare."

This was getting tedious. He waited two months before returning to the subject, this time inviting a conservative Wilson scholar to the show. "Woodrow Wilson and FDR captured the Democrats for this progressive movement and took us fundamentally off the tracks that our founders had built and moved us into another direction. True or false?"

"Very true," the author answered.

But how? "You get the progressives on both sides who brought you the income tax, forced sterilization of the inmates, eugenics, Prohibition," Beck later explained.

Wilson actually vetoed the Volstead Act, which was written to enforce Prohibition. But no matter. Beck was unstoppable in his anti-Wilson war. He even found a way to blame Wilson for the Japanese attack on Pearl Harbor—

twenty years after Wilson left office and seventeen years after his death.

"You want to know why they bombed us? It didn't come out of the blue. You know why? Because Woodrow Wilson told England you need to align yourself with us and not Japan. And so we humiliated Japan." Beck's unassailable conclusion: "The Progressives started it, then pretended it was a big surprise."

It was probably the most creative reading of twentieth-century history since *Animal House*. Remember when Bluto asks his fraternity brothers: "Was it over when the Germans bombed Pearl Harbor? Hell, no!"

"Germans?" asks Otter.

"Forget it, he's rolling," says Boon.

"And it ain't over now," Bluto concludes. " 'Cause when the going gets tough, the tough get going."

Beck, too, was rolling—although his version of Bluto's phrase once came out on air like this: "We're Americans. When the tough gets going, that's when we usually arrive."

Whatever.

One conclusion at which Beck had clearly arrived was that Wilson was to blame for all manner of problems. "Under Woodrow Wilson," he announced one night, "we have 30,000 people put in jail during World War I for speaking out." He came back later in the show to say the number was actually "2,000, 3,000 people." Actually, more like

1,100 were jailed or fined under the Sedition Act of 1918, which was indeed a stain on Wilson's presidency. But among those imprisoned was Eugene Debs—the Socialist Party leader. Why would progressives, who supposedly wanted to lead the country toward socialism, jail the most prominent Socialist of the day?

Beck left that mystery unsolved. He was too busy finding Wilson's evil fingerprints elsewhere—even in Obama's use of policy "czars" in the White House. "The presidents have had czars for a long time. Woodrow Wilson, he was spooky," pronounced Beck. "Woodrow Wilson, he was a progressive just like this president. He talked about, you know, ways to get things done by going around Congress . . . Guess what? This is a progressive in the White House. That's what he's doing. He's going right around Congress. When are you going to wake up, Congress?"

Aha! Beck had begun to place the Wilsonian noose around the Obamian neck. Finally, on September 18, 2009, he found a tree for the hanging—the "Tree of Revolution." The host illustrated this tree on his ubiquitous chalkboard, which he uses to help viewers understand his points when they become too convoluted, which is most of the time.

"I'm going to show you something that I think will help tie everything that we've been talking about for the past few months, tie it all together," Beck said, introducing the tree on the chalkboard.

The tree looked to be a sturdy oak. Buried in the ground where the trunk sat was Woodrow Wilson. To the left of Wilson, also in the roots of the tree, was Che Guevara, the Marxist revolutionary. To the right of Wilson was Saul Alinsky, the late social radical.

Wilson, along with Che and Alinsky, were the Miracle-Gro of the Tree of Revolution.

Farther up the trunk was SDS—Students for a Democratic Society, the 1960s group that protested the Vietnam War. Above SDS were the words "Cloward and Piven." This rather obscure reference was to two Columbia University academics who in 1966 wrote a *Nation* magazine article that Beck finds objectionable.

On the left branch of the tree were the Service Employees International Union (SEIU) and the ACORN community group, represented, appropriately enough, by an acorn. On the right branch of the tree were Bill Ayers, Obama's "terrorist" pal; Van Jones, an Obama adviser Beck had just driven to resign; and something called "the Apollo Alliance." Beneath that—a low-hanging fruit?—was Obama adviser Valerie Jarrett.

Now it started getting complicated. Jeff Jones, who with Bill Ayers was part of the Weather Underground, is an adviser to Apollo—where Van Jones used to work! And Jeff and Van have the same last name—Jones!

Various dollar bills were pasted to the branches on the

chalkboard, forming leaves. "All these places where there are dollar bills, George Soros has his hands in it," Beck explained.

Beck began to unveil more elements of the conspiracy shown on the Tree of Revolution:

The Apollo Alliance, funded by George Soros, wrote Obama's stimulus bill! Apollo's Jeff Jones, along with Obama friend Bill Ayers, "came right from SDS," which is "code language for Marxism," and formed the Weather Underground, responsible for "blowing up the Pentagon"! (Actually, the group blew up a bathroom, but still . . .). ACORN founder Wade Rathke is connected to SEIU because "his brother Dale is at SEIU, we think." (SEIU denies this, and there is no evidence for it, but stay with him.) The whole bunch of them were inspired by Richard Cloward and Frances Piven, who wanted to "get everyone on welfare, just start racking up the bills so the American financial system would eventually collapse."

"Look who the president has!" an agitated Beck continued, following the chalkboard tree trunk. "Wade Rathke, right up the tree! Dale [Rathke], right up the tree! Bill Ayers, right up the tree! Jeff Jones, right up the tree!"

It was brilliant. In summary, Woodrow Wilson mated with an Argentine revolutionary and a Chicago radical, gave birth to a 1960s antiwar group and a pair of Columbia academics, who in turn spawned ACORN, the SEIU, the

Apollo Alliance, the Weather Underground, George Soros, and Barack Obama!

The implications were astounding! Woodrow Wilson is Obama's grandfather! Obama's cousins bombed the Pentagon! Valerie Jarrett is George Soros's sister! And the White House has been taken over by South American revolutionaries!

"We've told you that these are radicals," Beck announced as he outlined this airtight case. "We've told you that there are communists, Marxists, revolutionaries all around this president."

And it's all Wilson's fault for being the fertilizer of the Tree of Revolution. No wonder Beck was so mad at him.

Beck continued his attack. "Our kids are still being taught that Woodrow Wilson and FDR were these lovable presidents who were so great," he complained the next month. "Woodrow Wilson was the biggest racist president [who] ever served."

By January 2010, Beck wasn't just accusing Wilson's progeny of planting bombs; he fingered Wilson himself as the bomber. "I saw what they set up," he told viewers. "They started a hundred-year time bomb. They planted it in the early 1900s, mainly with this guy, Woodrow Wilson, one evil SOB, bad dude! . . . He thought the American people were just too stupid to understand. Does any of this sound like today?"

The similarities between Obama and Wilson became unmistakable—to Beck.

"I haven't seen anything in American history like what is being played out right now unless I go back to the early twentieth century with Woodrow Wilson and the early progressive movement . . . Prohibition, the Fed, income tax, and the power grab that happened around 1915. True or false?"

"True," said Beck's obliging guest, author Thomas Sowell. This was the correct answer.

"Correct me if I'm wrong in any of this. The progressives love dictators . . . and most importantly, they were also for eugenics, which led to the Holocaust."

"Absolutely," said the guest. Right again!

Wilson's progressives went to ground, Beck argued, then suddenly reemerged decades later. "While this country has been asleep, we have been co-opted. There are now more than eighty members of the Progressive Caucus."

Beck called in an expert for confirmation. "You've talked to me more about the progressive movement, which is the disease," Beck said. "Would you agree it is the disease?"

"It is the disease," the guest dutifully agreed. "They saw the Constitution as a roadblock to their grand designs for bigger government and they set about to dismantle it beginning with Woodrow Wilson."

"If you look at Woodrow Wilson," another guest offered,

"you can draw a straight line intellectually . . . to Barack Obama today."

The list of Wilson's evils was long. His high taxes caused a depression. And, decades before George W. Bush was even born, Wilson lied in order to coerce the nation into war. "Woodrow Wilson ran for reelection and he just barely won. And he said we're never going to go to war in Europe. Lo and behold, just a few months later, World War I!"

Didn't that have something to do with Germany sinking American ships? Never mind. Just stay with him.

The real point, Beck argued, is this: "Today is 1917."

Accordingly, Americans had better brush up on their history. "I know you're busy," he pleaded with his viewers in March 2010. "The last thing you want to do is pick up a book and read about Woodrow Wilson—I hate this guy . . . But you're going to have to. You're going to have to learn history."

But for those who really don't have time, there's always the chalkboard. "Chalkboard, Tree of Revolution," Beck reminded viewers, turning to his arboreal diagram. "Look here, above Woodrow Wilson! SDS—this is where Bill Ayers came from, Van Jones, Dale Rathke, Wade Rathke. This was—this was, 'Let's blow things up,' and then Cloward and Piven said, 'No, no, no, let's try to just collapse the system . . .'"

In the Tree of Revolution, Beck was again out on a limb.

CHAPTER 10
SCALPS

＊＊＊

To those who doubt the power of Beck, two words provide ample refutation: Van Jones.

When forty-year-old Anthony "Van" Jones was named an adviser in the White House Council on Environmental Quality, few took notice. His appointment to the midlevel position was announced in a written statement by the CEQ director and kissed off in a 101-word brief by the Associated Press. The dispatch said Jones founded an "organization that promises environmentally friendly jobs to help lift people out of poverty" and was author of "the New York Times bestseller *The Green Collar Economy*."

That was true. But what it didn't mention—and what Obama White House officials didn't know—was that Jones had once been a communist. It wasn't a secret; Jones had been quite outspoken about it before changing his ways several years earlier. Obama aides figured the position was too junior to merit screening and vetting.

That was a big mistake.

Four months after Jones started work at the White House, he was discovered by Beck. Jones's ordeal began on July 23, 2009, as Beck was making the dubious proposition that everything Obama does is part of an effort to exact reparations for slavery. Beck then took viewers on a circuitous path that arrived at the door of Jones.

"Obama's new green czar, Van Jones, this is a guy who is a self-avowed communist, and he is in the Obama administration," Beck explained. "He spent six months in jail, came out a communist. Then he was a communist-anarchist radical. And then he decided—he found the eco-movement—and decided green is the new red. He then went on to become a green expert."

Some things Beck said were true, and some were complete fiction, but there was no way to know at the moment, because nobody had ever heard of Van Jones. Beck quickly moved on to a denunciation of green jobs, but the fun with Jones had only just begun.

Just five days after this first bite at Jones, Beck made his infamous claim that Obama has a "deep-seated hatred" for white people. As previously detailed, this led a group called Color of Change, cofounded by none other than Van Jones, to call for an advertiser boycott. The fact that Jones had left the group long before didn't seem to matter to Beck, who, a couple of weeks after the boycott began, went after Jones with new fervor.

Since then, Beck has rarely gone a week without mentioning Jones, and on average mentions him at least daily. In just over nine months (into the spring of 2010) Beck and his TV interlocutors invoked the name Van Jones an incredible 435 times. Long after Jones quit the White House in September 2009—driven out by Beck—he remained in Beck's view of the world as a central player in Obama conspiracies. Jones was a perfect villain for Beck: a man—a black man!—with proven ties to Obama and a long paper trail in radical politics. Best of all, he was unknown to the public, so—unlike Obama—Beck could define him any way he chose.

On August 24, a month after Beck introduced his viewers to the "communist" Jones, he essentially turned *The Glenn Beck Show* into *The Van Jones Show*. "Here is czar number one. The first stop is Van Jones," Beck began. He showed a video clip of poor quality featuring a profane Jones blasting oil companies. Another clip had him describing his job at the White House as "a community organizer inside the federal family."

Over piano music, Beck narrated. "Let's start at law school. Van Jones showed up wearing combat boots and holding a Black Panther book bag. He said of that period,

'If I had been in another country, I probably would have joined some underground guerrilla sect.' "

More Jones images followed.

A major turning point came in 1993 when he was arrested during the Rodney King riots. In jail he, quote, "met all of these young radical people of color, I mean, really radical—communists and anarchists. And it was, like, this is what I need to be a part of," end quote . . . Jones says, "By August, I was a communist." He spent the next ten years as a full-fledged radical, among other things founding a group called STORM, Standing Together to Organize a Revolutionary Movement, which held study groups in the Marxist and Lenin teachings.

For about seven minutes, Beck went on.

All of STORM's members developed a basic under-standing of and a commitment to revolutionary Marxist policies . . . The group particularly revered Mao Tse-tung . . . In 1999, Jones was arrested again while protesting the World Trade Organization. STORM dissolved three years later. He has since renounced black nationalism to focus on environ-mentalist issues . . .

"And why is it that such a committed revolutionary has made it so high into the Obama administration as one of his chief advisers?" Beck wanted to know, then bestowed a slogan on his prey: "Van Jones: Yes, still a revolutionary. Now, just a more effective, and, dare I say, powerful one." Beck said he asked the White House if it was "aware that Van Jones has this background in radical politics."

The White House, he said, responded that "Jones is entirely focused on one policy goal, building clean energy incentives." As Beck correctly observed, "That doesn't seem like an answer."

In truth, the White House had no idea about Jones, and Obama officials were in the worst possible place: at the mercy of Glenn Beck.

The drumbeat became daily. On August 25, Beck spoke of Jones as "a self-proclaimed radical, revolutionary communist—his words, not mine." He compared him to Venezuela's Hugo Chávez. "He's a communist, focused on what? Job creation."

The next night, Beck said the White House had "emailed several times and said 'stop calling Van Jones a czar.' They say he's a 'special adviser.'" Beck said nobody was refuting his claim that Jones was "a radical communist."

Actually, some were. Jones had given up his communism and turned into an avowed capitalist. "We cannot realistically proceed without a strong alliance between the best of the business world—and everyone else," he wrote in *The Green Collar Economy*. But the fact that he was once a communist was, for Beck's purposes, close enough.

Beck spoke in the present tense as he recited Jones's offenses to Bill O'Reilly: "Radical, radical. Believes Mao Tse-tung was a great guy. Wants an overthrow of the American system." He also said Jones "named his four-year-old son after a Marxist guerrilla out of Africa."

A few days later, Beck had "newly discovered audio and video" of Jones. The White House adviser, identified on-screen as "Self-Avowed Communist," could be heard saying, "This movement is deeper than a solar panel . . . We're going to change the whole system."

Then came video that Beck found of Jones saying "the white polluters and the white environmentalists are essentially steering poison into the people of color communities." He also played a clip of Jones mocking "clean coal" technology. "Or we could have unicorns pull our cars for us, you know," Jones said. "We could have the tooth fairy bring us our energy at night."

"Or we could have a self-proclaimed communist create jobs," Beck retorted. "Speaking of unicorns and fairies, what do they have in mind to replace 48 percent of our national energy source once they bankrupt it? Will Van Jones sprinkle pixie dust on giant windmills to make up the difference? . . . Will progressive pigs fly right out of

Van Jones's butt and pedal bicycles to power the turbines attached to our power grid?"

The forces of Beck had been unleashed. A Beck fan site, DefendGlenn.com, posted a grainy video of Jones recorded in February 2009, a month before he started at the White House. It had Jones saying "nobody belongs here but the Native American peoples" and, most damaging, Jones calling Republicans "assholes" for blocking Obama's agenda. "That's a technical, political science term." Added Jones: "I can be an asshole, and some of us who are not Barack Hussein Obama are going to have to get uppity."

The White House was losing its appetite for defending Jones. Trying to keep his job, Jones released a statement: "I apologize for the offensive words I chose to use during that speech. They do not reflect the views of this administration, which has made every effort to work in a bipartisan fashion, and they do not reflect the experience I have had since I joined the administration."

Beck's reply: Apology not accepted. The night after Jones's apology, Beck was back on the air with more on Jones. After thirty minutes of buildup and teasing, he unveiled his latest discovery. "He is also a 9/11 truther . . . After the 9/11 attacks, they demanded on their Web site, quote, 'a call for immediate inquiry into the evidence that suggests high-level government officials may have deliberately allowed the September 11th attacks to occur.' "

Jones's signature was on the truthers' petition. "So, on top of all of the radical progressive and communist nonsense coming from Obama's green jobs czar, Van Jones, you can now add, thinks the Bush administration blew up the World Trade Centers and covered it up . . . 9/11 truther, a guy believes that Bush intentionally killed 3,000 American citizens."

Jones didn't know it yet, but he was finished. The White House put out the weak defense that he "didn't carefully review" the petition before signing it. Jones asked that his name be removed from the petition. "I do not agree with this statement and it certainly does not reflect my views now or ever," he said in a statement, his second apology of the week.

His apology did nothing. The day after Beck's "truther" broadcast, Republican leaders demanded Jones's resignation. The next day, he resigned—angrily. "On the eve of historic fights for health care and clean energy, opponents of reform have mounted a vicious smear campaign against me. They are using lies and distortions to distract and divide," he complained. "I cannot in good conscience ask my colleagues to expend precious time and energy defending or explaining my past. We need all hands on deck, fighting for the future."

The White House washed its hands of Jones with a tepid thank-you-for-your-service statement.

Beck, for his part, began a victory lap that lasted the better part of a year.

Every couple of nights he would play a clip from a Jones video as part of a larger point about the Obama administration's communist tendencies. For example:

"We can't seem to shake the radical influence of former green jobs czar Van Jones, because it ain't just Van Jones."

"Once again, there's a budding scandal that is completely invisible to the people who do not watch Fox News. This joins the parade of such scandals as Van Jones."

"The 9/11 truther, Van Jones: Who got him into the White House?"

"The first chink in the armor was when Van Jones was forced to resign because of this program."

"We cannot let them disappear like Obama allowed Van Jones to disappear in the middle of the night, because Van Jones—I've got news for you, gang—is still in the system."

"This is Marx. This is Che. This is Van Jones."

Jones, for his part, landed a teaching job at Princeton's Woodrow Wilson School—named for the only person living or dead whom Beck seems to loathe more than Jones. "It's kind of a Glenn Beck Program five o'clock smart joke," Beck commented. "Woodrow Wilson and Van Jones—who would have seen that coming?" Of Jones's other position, with the Center for American Progress, Beck likened it to Tiger Woods "caught in bed with an exotic dancer and in response install[ing] a stripper pole right there in his guest-house."

The NAACP awarded the fallen Jones its President's Award, calling him an "American treasure" and arguing that "a defining trait of our country is our collective capacity to practice forgiveness and celebrate redemption."

At the awards ceremony, Jones had a reply to the man who brought him down. "To my fellow countryman, Mr. Glenn Beck: I see you and I love you, brother. I love you and you cannot do anything about it . . . Let's be one country."

"Implication here is that I don't love him," Beck replied on his show.

Now, where would somebody get that idea?

Months later, Jones delivered a surprisingly generous assessment of Beck:

Glenn Beck, seriously, recovering alcoholic. My father's an alcoholic. It's incredibly difficult to do what he's done, to be able to actually get sober. He is a father of a special-needs daughter about whom he speaks with great tenderness and great care. You don't see that very often. He's a heterosexual man who is willing to weep in public. That doesn't happen very often . . . I don't agree with him and I think he's using his genius and his talents in ways that are destructive to the country, but I love him as a person.

Beck's response was not quite so generous:

So the guy who was calling for a revolution, a communist revolution, a guy who has said that the
United States not only . . . blew up the World Trade
Center but also [that] the white people in America
are poisoning communities of color, he's now lov-
ing me and calling me a genius and saying that, you
know, he just disagrees? The problem with Van Jones
is that statement that he made, "I am more than
willing to drop the radical pose for the radical ends."
That makes it hard to trust anyone when he talks
about posing.

The acquisition of Van Jones's scalp filled Beck with
bloodlust. He was convinced the entire Obama administration was chock-full of Marxists, Maoists, and communists
of every stripe. All that he was lacking was evidence.

He set his "watch dogs"—his followers who search
the Internet for clues to fill out Beck's theories—to work
on more administration targets. "Van Jones was the tip of
the iceberg," he wrote in one message on Twitter. "Watch
Dogs: FIND EVERYTHING YOU CAN ON CASS SUNSTEIN,
MARK LLOYD AND CAROL BROWNER," he Tweeted. "Do
not link before burning to disc." The names were those of
three other Obama advisers on Beck's long hit list.

"This wasn't about Van Jones," he told his viewers after Jones had been forced out. "This is to try to figure out who the president of the United States is, by looking at the people he surrounded himself with." And the people he surrounded himself with, curiously, all seem to hate America.

Beck moved himself to tears as he spoke of the various and sundry Obama communists. "What I am telling you now is that there are Marxist revolutionaries who have dedicated themselves to principles that will destroy our nation as we know it!" he shouted. After his tears subsided, he went on: "I'm asking you to consider things that sound insane. But they're true."

Variations of that cry would go out every few days. "They are exposing themselves as the radical, revolutionary country-destroyers that they are," he said months later. "Because only one is going to be standing in the end—our country, or the progressives."

This was, of course, the very lowest form of political argument: describing your political opponents not just as opponents but as enemies of the nation. It's impossible to have a rational debate with a traitor who seeks to destroy the country. But, then again, rational debate wasn't exactly what Beck was going for.

Beck's first choice of an Obama administration target, even before Jones, had been a physicist by the name of John Holdren, who had taken a leave from Harvard's Kennedy

School to become director of the White House Office of Science and Technology Policy.

Holdren first came to Beck's attention after the Web site World Net Daily and other parts of the conservative blogosphere began to report that Holdren, more than three decades earlier, had written some very strange things. In a pattern that would repeat itself over and over again, Beck took the whispers from the dark corners of the Internet and splashed them in the mass media.

"The science czar," Beck told his viewers one night in July 2009, "once wrote with very little disapproval about using forced sterilization for population control."

"Just absolutely beyond the pale," said Beck's guest, from the conservative *National Review*. "As far as we know, he has never renounced."

"No, never," Beck concurred. He then read from Holdren's book: "The government might require only implantation of a contraceptive capsule to sterilize people," Beck read. "It must have no effect on members of the opposite sex, children and old people, and also pets or livestock."

Added Beck: "So, he doesn't mind making men sterile, as long as, you know, Fluffy isn't hurt."

"Sterilizing agents from drinking water," the guest contributed. "I mean, it's nuts." He added that "the man has signed his name to all of this."

A week later, Beck was after Holdren again. "We got

czars coming out our—they're shooting out of our butts," he said. "Czars like John Holdren who is—there is great evil happening in our country. Holdren has proposed forced abortions and putting sterilants in the drinking water to control population."

Proposing forced abortions and sterilizing agents in the drinking water? That *would* be evil—if it were true. But it wasn't.

Holdren did indeed coauthor a book in 1977 titled *Ecoscience*, a college textbook. And the book does indeed discuss "involuntary fertility control." But the authors didn't exactly endorse it. The book says that "some countries may ultimately have to resort to [such actions] unless current trends in birth rates are rapidly reversed by other means." It contained the part that Beck quoted, but it also said that "the risk of serious unforeseen side effects would, in our opinion, militate against the use of any such agent [as sterilants]." The authors said "a far better choice" would be to use "milder methods."

As for "forced abortions," they argued that, in a legal sense, "compulsory abortion could be sustained under the existing Constitution if the population crisis became sufficiently severe to endanger the society," but "few today consider the situation in the United States serious enough to justify compulsion."

No proposal for forced abortion here—just a textbook

legal analysis (albeit a dubious one) of this and every other possible population-control option.

But what Beck lacked in actual facts, he made up for with repetition—each time taking Holdren's argument further beyond what the textbook said. One night it was this: "He said that nowhere in the Constitution or the Declaration of Independence can you find the right to have any number of children." Two weeks later it was this: "He believes that we should have planetary control, you know, through the U.N." Several weeks later it was: "He also said maybe forced abortions would be good—you know, the kind they have in China. Has he ever denounced these methods? No, no."

★ ★ ★

However hard Beck swung at Holdren, he just couldn't dislodge him from his White House job. The charges wouldn't stick, and so, except for the occasional mention of Holdren, Beck moved on.

He had only modestly more success with the next name on his hit list: Harvard law professor Cass Sunstein, who, like Van Jones and Holdren, came to Beck's attention after first becoming the subject of attacks on the far-right Web site World Net Daily.

Sunstein had been nominated to head the Office of Information and Regulatory Affairs (Beck called the position the "regulatory czar," though it was a Senate-confirmed position that existed long before the Obama presidency).

Sunstein's appointment was, if anything, a nod to conservatives on Obama's part. Sunstein had backed John Roberts to be chief justice of the Supreme Court and supported the Supreme Court's Heller decision, voiding Washington, D.C.'s handgun ban.

But Beck had a different view. He determined that Sunstein was unfit to hold office because of his views on . . . pets? "Wait until you meet this guy," Beck said on his Fox show. He "believes in giving legal rights to livestock, wildlife, and pets. So, your pet can have an attorney file a lawsuit against you. When my pet starts to talk, he can call an attorney. Human rights for livestock? This is not the America I grew up in or you grew up in."

As Sunstein's confirmation vote in the Senate approached, Beck stepped up his attack. August 25, 2009: "Cass Sunstein . . . has also proposed that your dog be allowed to have an attorney in court." September 2: "He wanted your pet to have an attorney . . . If they could find out if rats suffer, and you're trying to trap rats or kick them out of your house, a rat could sue you."

This was, evidently, based on the introduction Sunstein and a coauthor wrote for a 2004 book on animal rights that they edited. In it, Sunstein and his coauthor actually argued something close to the opposite of what Beck charged: that states could enforce animal cruelty laws without declaring that animals could no longer be considered property.

"A state could dramatically increase enforcement of existing bans on cruelty and neglect without turning animals into persons, or making them into something other than property," they wrote. "A state could do a great deal to prevent animal suffering, indeed carry out the central goals of the animal welfare program, without saying that animals cannot be owned. We could even grant animals a right to bring suit without insisting that animals are persons, or that they are not property. A state could certainly confer rights on a pristine area, or a painting, and allow people to bring suit on its behalf, without therefore saying that that area and that painting may not be owned."

Conservative writer David Frum judged Beck's interpretation of Cass's work to be "beyond sloppy, beyond ignorant, proceeding straight toward the deceptive."

But effective. Two Republican senators put "holds" on the nomination, blocking it from being considered by the Senate. Finally, Senate Democrats held a vote on September 9 to try to break the Republican filibuster—and Beck came on air just as the vote was approaching.

"It is supposed to happen—surprise, surprise, no coincidence in politics—in this hour," Beck said. "You can still call Washington and tell them 'no.'"

He repeated his grievances. Sunstein is, Beck said, "a

man who doesn't believe we should be eating meat . . . a man who believes that animals should be provided attorneys in the courts of law, a man who believes that everyone must be an organ donor, a man that believes that you should not be able to remove rats from your home if it causes them any pain.

"This is the lunatic fringe!" said Beck, who speaks with some authority on the subject.

But, as with Holdren, the charges didn't stick. The filibuster was broken, and the next day Sunstein was confirmed, 57–40. There have been, as of this writing, no attempts to ban hunting or meat eating or to give dogs or rats legal standing.

Beck could do nothing more than add Sunstein to his list of Obama officials planning a progressive/communist/socialist/fascist takeover of the country. His monologues became seasoned with phrases such as "Are you crazy, Cass?" and "Extreme radical Cass Sunstein" and "the most dangerous man in America."

★ ★ ★

But in Beck's mind there were many people vying for the title of most dangerous man or woman—and as luck would have it, they all worked for Barack Obama.

Carol Browner, a former Clinton administration official hired by Obama to advise him on climate issues, was a socialist, Beck determined. "Hard core," confirmed his guest, from *The National Review*.

This allegation stemmed from Browner's affiliation with the Commission for a Sustainable World Society, which was indeed organized by the Socialist International. But it includes such nonsocialists as former British prime ministers Gordon Brown and Tony Blair.

That was enough for Beck. "She was part of Socialists International. This is a group for global governance," he reported. "Socialist" became part of her title, as in "socialist energy czar." Every few weeks, Beck would remind viewers of her as he built the Obama socialist conspiracy on his chalkboard. "Carol Browner—she's a socialist," he would say, or "Carol Browner—you remember her. She's that socialist."

Beck's "watch dogs," meanwhile—those he reached on Twitter with a request to "find everything you can" on Browner, Sunstein, and Mark Lloyd—were beginning to come through for him. One sent him a video of Lloyd, "chief diversity officer," at the Federal Communications Commission, discussing Hugo Chávez's revolution in Venezuela. Lloyd described it as "really an incredible revolution." From this Beck deduced that the FCC lawyer "is a huge fan of the socialist/Marxist revolution in Venezuela."

Another Marxist! "I'm just on the beginning of my research of Mark Lloyd—but he strikes me as a Marxist,"

Beck proposed one night. Further, he concluded that Lloyd was "the man trying to silence free speech in America" and was "positively un-American."

"Have we found another Van Jones?" Beck teased his viewers one night. "I tell you the answer to that one is: No. We found someone, I believe, worse."

Beck's Kremlinology was starting to get complicated. There was a Marxist green-jobs adviser, a Marxist FCC official, a socialist energy adviser, an abortionist science adviser, and a regulatory adviser who wanted your dog to sue you. Enter Ron Bloom, whose Marxist/socialist credentials include a degree from Harvard Business School and work as an investment banker before he became an adviser to unions.

Soon after Obama named Bloom as an adviser on manufacturing policy, Beck started playing a clip of Bloom speaking: "We know that the free market is nonsense. We know that the whole point is to game the system, to beat the market or at least find someone who'll pay you a lot of money because they're convinced that there is a free lunch. We know this is largely about power, that it is an adults-only, no-limit game. We kind of agree with Mao that political power comes largely from the barrel of a gun. And we get it that if you want a friend, you should get a dog."

With that cynical take on the system, Bloom joined "the radicals the president has placed around himself," according to Beck. "Why," he asked another night, "do you think there are so many Maoists hanging around the White House?"

An excellent question. One explanation was that Obama was, as Beck alleged, a communist who stealthily stocked his administration with secret admirers of Red China. The other possibility was that Beck, with his Internet-combing "watchdogs," was turning any stray remark by any of the ten thousand political appointees in the Obama administration into a communist manifesto.

This second possibility gained some weight when Beck turned his sights on Anita Dunn, the White House communications director who had used that perch to criticize Fox News. Dunn was not your typical communist: She advised corporations, worked for former Senate leader Tom Daschle, and helped to run basketball great Bill Bradley's presidential campaign. But Beck saw her as a Maoist. His evidence: a high school graduation speech she gave.

"The third lesson and tip actually comes from two of my favorite political philosophers: Mao Tse-tung and Mother Teresa, not often coupled together, but the two people that I turn to most to basically deliver a simple point, which is, you're going to make choices," Dunn told the kids. She recalled Mao in 1947 saying, "You fight your war and I'll fight mine." And she recalled Mother Teresa saying, "Go find your own Calcutta."

It's not terribly uncommon for an American to quote Mao; John McCain has often observed that "in the words of Chairman Mao, it's always darkest before it's totally black." But Beck pounced, particularly on the "favorite political philosophers" bit. Dunn insisted she was joking—a reasonable proposition because neither the dictator nor the humanitarian quite qualifies as a philosopher—but Beck was convinced he had found another communist.

"It's not funny. It's not even close to funny," he responded on a later show.

Beck got out his red hotline—the one for which only the White House supposedly has the number. Dunn, he alleged, is one of a few White House officials who "worship Chairman Mao." By way of proof, he added: "Just call me if you don't have an altar in your bedroom." The phone didn't ring—it was true!

Beck liked this form of proof. "They won't challenge—they won't call me!" he exulted with his red phone on the set. "Communists, revolutionaries, socialists, Marxists, followers of Chairman Mao appointed by Obama to the executive branch in positions of the government—call, call me! Explain it, explain it any other way."

Before and after Dunn left the White House (she was there on a temporary basis for the first months of the Obama presidency), Beck continued to mau-mau the Maoists (sometimes even accompanied by photographs of executions and child labor in China): "Mao-loving Anita Dunn . . . one of her favorite political philosophers is Mao . . . the Mao fan, Anita Dunn . . . preaching the virtues of Mao . . . The Chairman Mao–lover, lizard lady, Anita Dunn . . . a follower of Mao . . . singing the praises of Chairman Mao . . . Every time I see an interview with her I wait for her tongue to come out. She's spooky. I expect, like, lasers to shoot out of her eyes."

★ ★ ★

In fairness, Beck doesn't claim that everybody who works for Obama is a communist. Some of them are fascists. One night, he discussed Nazi propagandist Joseph Goebbels, then added: "I'm going to show you the beginning of something that should scare the living daylights out of you. It is propaganda in America."

The conservative Web site Breitbart.com had posted a recording of a teleconference in which the communications director for the National Endowment for the Arts, Yosi Sergant, seemed to be encouraging artists to produce work that supports the Obama volunteer-service agenda.

Sergant, who during the campaign popularized the iconic "Hope" image of Obama, said on the call: "I would encourage you to pick something, whether it's health care, education, the environment. There are four key areas that the corporation has identified as the areas of service."

Beck interviewed the man who recorded the teleconference. The charges caused an uproar on Capitol Hill, and within days Sergant was gone. "We played the tapes of the call with Yosi Sergant," Beck celebrated, "and Yosi Sergant had to step down."

But after a year and a half of hunting, Beck had only two scalps to show for his efforts, the relatively minor figures of Sergant and Jones. He began to cast his net wider. One night he went after a Canadian named Maurice Strong, who works with the United Nations. "I need videos and anything you can find on Maurice Strong and you send it to us right away," he told his watchdogs. Beckoning to his White House hotline, he said, "The reason why this phone is not ringing now is because there are phone calls being made and they are scouring the Internet. They are sanitizing and taking it all off."

That was a bit obscure, but Beck was out of good targets. He finally settled on exposing people who had not yet been appointed by Obama. "You mark my words," he said after Justice John Paul Stevens announced his retirement from the Supreme Court. "A radical is coming. Sotomayor, I'm sorry, gang, but she's a radical. He's going to pick another radical. I mean, if he's smart, he will find a gay, handicapped, black woman who's an immigrant. She could say, 'I hate America, I want to destroy America,' and that way they'll only be able to say, 'Why do you hate gay, immigrant, black, handicapped women?'"

Not only was Beck a first-rate communist hunter, but he

was also a clairvoyant: The nominee had yet to be named, but Beck already knew she wanted to destroy America.

And, sure enough, he was right. Just a few days after Elena Kagan was nominated, Beck reported that "Kagan happens to be a big fan of Cass Sunstein . . . who I maintain is the most dangerous man in America, okay?"

This can only mean one thing: Kagan, too, wants dogs to sue their owners.

CHAPTER 11

HEY, KIDS, LET'S PUT ON A SHOW!

· ·

Glenn Beck was burning mad.

He was mad that President Obama was making nice to Somali pirates. "They're sending over a hostage negotiator. Yes, I hope we're bringing them some hot cocoa." (Navy snipers shot the pirates dead and freed their captive unharmed.)

Beck was also burning mad that the economy was improving—after President Obama's stimulus bill had taken effect. Damn! "Retailers saw a better than expected number today," he reported. "Stores including Walmart, Target, and Costco expect to boost their sales for April. Due to Easter," he added, to make clear it was Jesus' doing, not Obama's.

And Beck was really, really, really mad that Obama dared to say he'd like to see immigration reforms taken up by Congress. Slurring like a drunk, Beck mocked Obama: "I'm pretty much done, not a lot more to do, you know. I got all those things done. You know, why don't I work on immigration reform?"

This drove Beck to the point of . . . televised arson.

"Maybe I'm alone," he continued, "but I think it would be just faster if they just shot me in the head." Like a Somali pirate, perhaps. "You know what I mean? How much more can—how much more can he disenfranchise all of us?"

With that, Beck introduced his guest—Bill Schulz from Fox's *Red Eye* program—and then, picking up a large red gas can, proceeded to pour the contents on Schulz. With each dousing from the can, he called out Obama's sins, the way Jews, during the Passover seder, recite the ten plagues that were visited on Egypt.

"Let's say Bill is the average American here and I'm President Obama. This is the way I feel."

"The only fat they cut out is national defense!" (Obama's budget had the largest Pentagon allocation in history.)

"We have growing Social Security. We have Medicare, Medicaid obligations, right?"

"We are buried under 1.25 quadrillion dollars in debt."

"Obama is apologizing to the Frenchy French for our arrogance."

"He's bowing to the Saudi Arabian king."

"He's also closing Gitmo and letting the terrorists onto the streets."

"The Congressional Black Caucus met with Fidel Castro . . . Ninety-three percent of [the] Cuban labor force works for the state. Sound familiar? . . . Seven abortions for every ten babies born in Cuba. Sure, sounds like a vacation in Disneyland to me."

"Obama wants to legalize the illegal aliens."

Schulz obediently shivered, hyperventilated, and rubbed his eyes as the fluid covered his head and shoulders. On-screen, a cartoon Beck appeared with the words "Don't worry, it's water, I promise."

"Do you have any matches?" the host asked. A production worker on the set brought him a pack.

"President Obama, why don't you just set us on fire?" Beck asked. "For the love of Pete, what are you doing? . . . We didn't vote to lose the republic."

The match was lit and blown out without igniting Schulz. Beck continued the rant: "You're spending money that leads only to slavery! . . . We can disagree with each other on policies, but Good Lord Almighty, man, please. Some of us don't agree with all of the policies. We'd like to have a country left in the end of four years. No need to set us on fire."

Beck turned to his other guest, who happened to be the governor of Texas, Rick Perry. "Governor, you're regretting being on this program at this point, are you not, sir?"

"Not at all, Glenn Beck. I'm proud to be with you."

Beck later explained: "I just want to show you, kids, water, not gasoline. I was—I was actually told by our legal department, 'Glenn, you can't just do that, you've got to'—I said, 'Yes, this is why our country is so screwed up if I got to actually say, that wasn't really gasoline, kids.' Don't do that at home. That would be really, really bad."

Moments later, he had an addendum for the kids: "By the way, that was absolutely high-octane jet fuel."

* * *

Love Glenn Beck or hate Glenn Beck, there is no denying the man is an entertainment genius. His props, his costumes, and his overall shtick are the worst, which is to say the best, in the business.

The man who makes tens of millions of dollars from his TV, radio, and Internet interests likes to wear blue jeans and sneakers on the set along with his jacket and tie. The man who skipped college is rarely on air without his trusty chalkboard so he can give a professorial illustration of his points and paste up photographs of those whose scalps he would claim. The comedian Jon Stewart alleged that the populist Beck travels with two chalkboard "caddies" when he takes his show on the road.

Stewart obviously doesn't appreciate the high degree of risk involved in using a chalkboard for a prop on live television. One night, Beck was employing his chalkboard to find a code in various words he associated with Obama ("left," "international," "graft," "revolutionaries") and, cracking the code, spelled the word "oligarch" on the board. Except he wrote "OLIGARH." Beck had forgotten to write the C-word. (Communists? No: czars.)

That's life on the high wire, and Beck likes it there. One night he'll come out with inflated rubber balls for a round of dodgeball. Another night he'll have an actor dress up as Thomas Paine and read Beck's words as if they were a modern-day version of Paine's famous *Common Sense*. Or he'll pull out his red "Mao hotline" phone and wait for President Obama to refute Beck's accusation that the White House is a den of communists.

The night after *Avatar* director James Cameron called him a "fucking asshole," Beck went on air, put on some paper 3-D glasses, and scrolled through "The 'I Hate Glenn Beck' Club, featuring Keith Olbermann, Chris Matthews, *Law & Order*, the Playboy bunny, and now Cameron."

Some of the stunts go well beyond normal bounds of taste and demonstrate why Beck is no mere "rodeo clown." Consider his playful skit about poisoning the Speaker of the House. He had a person on the set wear a Pelosi mask, then passed a glass of red wine across the table. "You gonna drink your wine?" he asked. "I want you to drink it now. Drink it, drink it, drink it." Moments later, he added, "By the way, I put poison in your—no, I look forward to all the policy discussions that we're supposed to have."

At least he didn't boil the Speaker of the House in a pot of water.

Others were not so lucky. It was in September 2009, and Beck's show was tracking over the usual ground. He had the latest on the ACORN "weasels" who were "helping to start brothels with illegal thirteen-year-olds." He went after the Kennedys, George Soros, Barney Frank, the Service Employees International Union, the Apollo Alliance, the Tides Center, the Needmor Fund, Van Jones, the Rathke brothers, and many others, tying them all into an Obama conspiracy. "Sometimes I feel like Russell Crowe from *A Beautiful Mind,* trying to lay it out for you. But it's difficult to demonstrate because it is massive."

Or imaginary.

But tonight, Beck had something new to say, and a new way to illustrate things. He was going to explain why John McCain could have been even worse as president than Obama—because McCain, too, is a dreaded "progressive."

Beck turned to a steaming stainless-steel pot of water on the set. "Let me explain this to you using this boiling water here, and these little frogs. You know the old saying, if you put a frog into boiling water, he's going to jump right out because he's scalding hot. But if you place him in lukewarm water and gradually raise the temperature, the frog won't realize what is happening and die.

"Let me get the frogs," Beck continued, reaching his hand into an aquarium full of what appeared to be frogs hopping about. "Okay, all right," he said, eventually pulling one out and cupping it in his hands. "So you have the little frogs here."

And now to his point: "Barack Obama has galvanized the country, because of the sheer size of the bills he has proposed, and the number of the bills, the urgency that he has been placing on the bills. He has forced us to think and get involved. We have not—like John McCain—been boiled slowly. We have been tossed quickly into boiling water. And don't forget what happens when you throw them in. When you throw them in, frogs into boiling water—"

Beck at this point tossed his frog into the pot, and there was a long pause. No frog jumped from the pot. "Okay, forget the frog," he resumed. "I swear I thought they jumped right out but they don't."

Only then did Beck say the frog "was fake." He then asked his guest, former Bush administration official John Bolton, to verify the animal's inauthenticity. "I know PETA is going to be all over me," he said. "By the way, the whole thing with the whole boiling water and a frog—that's fable. It's not true. We knew before we did that. Ambassador, will you verify that it's a rubber frog, that's not a real frog?"

The former U.S. ambassador to the United Nations obliged. "Very rubber," he said.

"You didn't expect to be asked that question, did you?" Beck asked.

It was the closest Beck had come to the truth all night.

★ ★ ★

Beck's show devolves into Animal Planet more often than you might think. Months after the frog sacrifice, Beck got rabid over Joe Biden's use of an old Sherlock Holmes line to say the administration hadn't wasted stimulus funds. "As Joe puts it, the dog so far at least hasn't barked," Obama said.

Beck played this on a big screen—and began to bark. It came out as a terrier's yap but quickly progressed to slobbering Doberman. "Dog hasn't barked?" he repeated. "It's like a pack of wild Cujos, ripping up the flesh of the American people. We've given you a dozen examples over the past year, stimulus debacles . . . Oh wait, here's my favorite: lawn mowers that magically created fifty jobs."

Beck let out a maniacal laugh, then turned to the screen and barked some more.

But if the dog and the frog were not real, the fish almost certainly was. It began with Beck pulling on some latex gloves. "I've got the blue gloves, because I thought they went nicely with my eyes," he said in an effeminate voice. He struggled with the prop. "These are the worst gloves ever! We couldn't get the stuff with, like, the baby powder in them? These are government gloves! They don't fit, look."

He finally got the gloves on. "Okay, here's what I want to show you," he began. "This is the dumbest damn show on air." No argument was offered to contradict this, but it wasn't the point Beck was going to make. He was going to talk about "Larry, the dead fish."

Beck placed a copy of the *New York Times* in front of him. He took a foot-long fish out of a bucket. "Meet my friend Larry, the dead fish," the host said. "Here he is. Hello, Larry."

"Hello, America," Larry the dead fish replied, borrowing a deep voice from Beck.

"Larry is here for the one reason that—Larry! Whew, Larry. Wow, Larry stinks. Larry is the dead fish that nobody wanted you to see," Beck continued. "Larry was printing up money last week. That's what he was doing."

Beck began to fold the newspaper around Larry, calling out the various distractions that prevented Americans from noticing that Larry the dead fish had been printing money last week. Obama's NCAA brackets: "Did you hear about his brackets? I loved his brackets." The AIG hearing: "Boy, that was really making me angry." Obama on Jay Leno: "It was just crazy."

Larry was now wrapped in newspaper. "All of that was to cover up the dead, stinky fish, the dead, stinky fish that nobody wanted you to pay any attention to: the fact that we were printing our own money and monetizing our debt."

★ ★ ★

There is a prop for every occasion, every enemy. A pipe to smoke while imitating liberal eggheads, a 1950s television to show an old clip from *The Music Man*, a desk to put his feet on while watching some video, and a swastika or hammer-and-sickle emblem to hold up as needed. To illustrate the proliferation of "radicals" in the Obama administration, he played a game of Connect Four against himself on the set. "We have Buffy and Yosi and we have Valerie, right? And then we have Barack Obama," Beck explained, putting four red checkers together—apparently not realizing that four yellow pieces had already been connected. He had better luck illustrating the corporate takeover of the United States by replacing the stars on the flag with the emblems of General Electric, General Motors, Walmart, Citibank, and others.

But Beck's populist assault on the Fortune 500 went only so far. When the topic turned to Andy Stern, former head of the Service Employees International Union, the prop was a baseball bat. Beck talks like a good ol' boy as he describes how the union bosses will beat up on corporations. "Hey, maybe we can just give him the name and address of every executive in American business and provide Andy and his goons with, you know, free baseball bats," he once said, brandishing the wood and even taking a practice swing. "You know that way they can just beat those company heads into submission. Metaphorically speaking. Of course no union thug would ever use something like that."

During an SEIU segment on another show, Beck portrayed Stern as a Mafia boss by playing a clip from *The Godfather*: "Luca Brasi sleeps with the fishes." (Not to be confused with Larry, the dead fish.) He then held up a shirt that said "Marxist" for White House adviser Van Jones, one that said "I [heart] Mao" for Anita Dunn, and for Stern, a T-shirt that said, "I Wanted to Overthrow the Government in the 1960's and All I Got Was This Lousy T-shirt."

During another show, Beck had workers in the Fox control room wear purple SEIU shirts, posing as goons. His staff got another dress-up day when Beck had them wear white lab coats and stand with him as he pointed to his chalkboard, where there was an illustration about how the whole world was becoming more socialist, "going for an even more oppressive and bloated government." Beck beckoned to his white coats. "The doctors know. I mean, they actually don't but having them stand here makes it seem like I'm right, doesn't it? Worked for Barack Obama. Why isn't it working for me?" The "doctors" stood silently, arms folded on chests.

When it appeared that the White House wasn't getting

the message that the stimulus plan wasn't working, Beck tried to amplify his message—by using a bullhorn on the set. To dramatize White House adviser Dunn's speech to high school students praising Mao, Beck invited a parent of one of the private-school children who heard the speech on the show to criticize Dunn. He had the father shot in silhouette, as if he were in the witness protection program, and distorted his voice so he sounded like Alvin and the Chipmunks. "Concerned Parent," the father was labeled on-screen.

"Mao would have preferred to silence the opposition by putting a bullet to the back of the head," the concerned parent/chipmunk said. "There are subtle ways to do it, and I think we're seeing it right now."

Such as dousing people with gasoline on TV?

Still, no chipmunks, fish, frogs, or dogs compare to the strange animals viewers saw on their screens one evening in July 2009. It began as one of Beck's fairly common rants against AmeriCorps, the community service program created by Bill Clinton and embraced by Obama.

"Do you remember when Barack Obama was on the campaign trail and he said, 'Oh I'm going to have an army of people in America and they'll be better financed than the military'?"

No, we don't remember that, but go on.

"I think AmeriCorps is part of that army," Beck explained. "And they—you know, I got the pledge and I was going to read it to you, but I thought, you know, I can't really read it to you, you know, sitting here like this."

With that, Beck jumped up from his desk and ripped off his jacket to reveal a full lederhosen ensemble: the knickers, the long socks, and the vest.

"I mean, to really go for it, I mean, to really do the AmeriCorps pledge, I think you have to be dressed like this. I think—I think you have to stand up and take your pledge."

He raised his hand and made a three-finger salute. He pledged: "I will get things done for America, to make our people safer, and smarter, and healthier. I will bring Americans together to strengthen our communities. Faced with apathy, I will take action. Faced with conflict, I will seek common ground. Faced with adversity, I will persevere. I will carry this commitment with me this year and beyond. I am an AmeriCorps member, and I will get things done."

Beck then broke into the song "Edelweiss" from *The Sound of Music*.

This performance earned the host a curtain call on Bill O'Reilly's show.

"Why the German outfit?" O'Reilly asked. "Why the Edelweiss? Why? This is AmeriCorps; this is America."

"Yes, I don't know," Beck answered. "I think it's about time that we used ridicule in this country."

"Who are you ridiculing? The Germans? The Ameri-Corps people?"

Beck explained that "if Rahm Emanuel gets his way,"

AmeriCorps "will be required service" for eighteen- to twenty-four-year-olds. There are no such plans for the program to be anything other than voluntary.

O'Reilly, usually in sync with Beck on philosophy, told him that "I'm not with you on the AmeriCorps."

O'Reilly later in the interview posed a reasonable question. "You do a lot of this kind of whacked-out stuff, the dancing with the lederhosen and interviewing yourself. Do you run a risk that some people are just going to dismiss the serious stuff that you're doing, the important points you're trying to make, because of the burlesque?"

"Yes, I do run that risk," Beck retorted. "But have you seen the ratings at 5 P.M.? Okay? [You] don't get those ratings at 5 P.M. by being Charlie Rose."

"I have to say that when I saw this in my office," O'Reilly said of the lederhosen episode, "I thought you were back on the sauce."

"It could happen at any time," Beck replied.

"Number two, I said to myself, is this the Hitler Youth thing he's doing? You know, because the Hitler Youth had the little short pants."

"Yes, but that's lederhosen there. That's completely different."

"Beck, I think it was the Hitler Youth thing," O'Reilly charged.

"I don't know what you're talking about, Bill O'Reilly."

Good thing Beck didn't have a gas can with him.

CHAPTER 12
PAGING AGENT MULDER

Glenn Beck woke up on the morning of March 3, 2009, and took a walk out onto a grassy knoll. He went on *Fox & Friends*, the Fox News morning show, and spoke words that, until that moment, had been confined to shows such as *The X-Files*, not cable news. He said it just might be true that the Obama administration's Federal Emergency Management Agency was staffing and maintaining concentration camps to imprison political dissenters as part of a plan to suspend the Constitution.

"We are a country that is headed toward socialism, totalitarianism, beyond your wildest imagination," he proffered. "I wanted to debunk these FEMA camps. I'm tired of hearing about them. You know about them. I'm tired of hearing about them. I wanted to debunk them. We've now for several days done research on them. I can't debunk them."

In fact, he suggested, he seemed to believe in the camps

himself. "If you trust our government, it's fine," he continued. "If you have any kind of fear that we might be heading towards a totalitarian state: Look out. Buckle up. There's something going on in our country that is—ain't good."

By the time Beck walked onto the set that evening for his 5 P.M. show, something weird had happened. He decided to clam up. Probably something involving Lee Harvey Oswald and the Trilateral Commission.

"I was going to talk about it today, but as I came in this morning and then I went into my office and I was looking at all the research that are being compiled, and it wasn't complete," he explained. "And I am not willing to bring something to you that is half-baked. If these things exist, that's bad, and we will cover it. If they don't exist, it's irresponsible to not debunk this story."

But given that Beck had already said he couldn't debunk the story about the U.S. Department of Concentration Camps, this comment only added to the intrigue, and implied more validity to the rumor. "We have an independent group on this program looking into it, turning over every stone," the host said. "I am going to bring you this story. This program is not beholden—This is going to drive the conspiracy theorists crazy. They're making me say this. Help!—this program is not beholden to anybody. We answer to ourselves. I answer to me. I lost sleep last night worrying about this story, thinking about this story, and wanted to make sure I got it right."

As a teaser, though, Beck said there was news that "fits together like a puzzle" and "it all adds up to government control." He then introduced his guest, libertarian former presidential candidate Ron Paul, who added to the suspicion:

"FEMA is already very, very powerful and they overrule [local authorities] when they go in on emergencies. So in some ways, they can accomplish what you might be thinking about setting up camps. And they don't necessarily have to have legislation, you know, to do the things that we dread, but it's something that deserves attention."

"Right," Beck said. "And I want to make it very clear: I'm not fearing these things are happening."

No, he was just saying he "can't debunk" the allegation that they were, in fact, happening—and that was all many on the far right needed to confirm their belief that Obama was seeking to suspend the Constitution and imprison them for disagreeing with him.

Beck might as well have issued a call to arms to the dormant militia movement: The Obama administration is coming to get you. It was a case study in how he has brought the far-out fringes of the Internet into the mainstream in a way no other person in the news business has done.

Still, there was a delicious irony in Beck's elevation of the concentration camp conspiracy theory to legitimate news story. To the extent anybody in the U.S. government did contemplate such a scheme, it was none other than Beck's colleague at Fox News, Ollie North.

The FEMA concentration camp story has floated around for a quarter century or more. The closest it ever came to reality was in 1987, when the Iran-Contra investigation was under way and the *Miami Herald* published a breathless story:

REAGAN ADVISERS RAN "SECRET" GOVERNMENT

President Reagan's top advisers have operated a virtual parallel government outside the traditional Cabinet departments and agencies almost from the day Reagan took office, congressional investigators and administration officials have concluded.

Investigators believe that the advisers' activities extended well beyond the secret arms sales to Iran and aid to the contras now under investigation.

Lt. Col. Oliver North, for example, helped draw up a controversial plan to suspend the Constitution in the event of a national crisis, such as nuclear war, violent and widespread internal dissent or national opposition to a U.S. military invasion abroad.

Aha! It was Colonel North, in the eighties, with the secret FEMA plan. And now he's hosting Fox's *War Stories*.

The *Herald* reported that North's idea involved a "secret contingency plan that called for . . . turning control of the United States over to FEMA, appointment of military commanders to run state and local governments and declaration of martial law during a national crisis."

This, in turn, was similar to a plan drafted by the Nixon administration, in 1970, which proposed a declaration of martial law if there were an uprising by black militants; at least 21 million African Americans would be placed in "assembly centers or relocation camps."

North's brainstorm was shot down by cooler heads in the Reagan administration. The colonel himself, in congressional testimony, denied advocating such a plan and said the government had adopted no such plan.

But the story still proved embarrassing, winding up as Soviet propaganda; the Russian news agency Tass reported on plans to suspend the Constitution "in the interests of protecting the rears of the aggressive policy of the military-industrial complex."

It was eventually forgotten, except among the conspiracy theorists. In the 1998 *X-Files* movie, Agent Fox Mulder was told that "FEMA allows the White House to suspend constitutional government upon declaration of a national emergency. It allows creation of a non-elected government. Think about that, Agent Mulder."

During the Bush years, when Michael "Brownie" Brown's FEMA couldn't handle a hurricane, much less the secret imprisonment of millions of political dissenters, the conspiracy theory didn't gain much traction. But then came Obama's inauguration, and Beck's arrival at Fox News. It was time for *The X-Files* to meet mainstream journalism.

Even a number of conservatives were appalled. "What the hell is going on at Fox News?" former Bush speechwriter David Frum wrote in a blog post after Beck's "can't debunk" moment. Frum also wasn't pleased to see that Beck, during an hour-long "televangelical special" on Fox the week before, had given each audience member what Frum said was a book written by a John Bircher and a "grand fantasist of theories about secret conspiracies between capitalists and communists to impose a one-world government under the control of David Rockefeller."

Apparently Beck couldn't debunk this one-world-government conspiracy, either.

"Are we headed for one world government?" he asked at the top of a later show, in October 2009. "America, if you believe this country is great but you—you're not really into that whole one world government thing, watch out— because the masks are coming off."

Beck alleged that White House officials were trying to "fundamentally transform this country into something revolutionary, almost Venezuelan in nature." He predicted that the government would fail, and "mark my words, it's the IMF or the U.N. Government and even bigger government will come to the rescue."

The night's topic: global warming. Beck's guest, a conservative British gadfly known as Lord Christopher Monckton, had been invited on to talk about his conspiracy theory that, as Beck put it, "is on fire on the Internet."

From Copenhagen, Monckton said, "A treaty will be signed that will, for the first time, create a world government with powers to intervene directly in the economy and in the environmental affairs of individual nations."

"What page is the global government on" in the treaty? Beck asked.

"Right. You go to Annex 1, Paragraph 38."

The other guest, former Bush adviser John Bolton, tried to inject some reason into the proceedings. He pointed out, correctly, that countries were "not prepared to sign on" to the sort of thing Monckton was talking about.

"With respect," Monckton replied, "I think we are heading here for what could be a global government."

Beck sided with his conspiracy-minded guest. "I really believe we have a group of radicals in the White House now, and in and around Washington, that are pushing for redistributive wealth, Marxism, socialism, global government," he said. "I mean it's all there."

In the end, neither a global government nor anything of substance emerged from the Copenhagen talks.

Developing the world-government-takeover panic, Beck has relied on the work of the kindred spirits at the far-right Web site World Net Daily. On May 18, 2010, for example, Beck appeared on *Fox & Friends* to deliver word that "we are moving into a global community" and that "there is global governance coming to the planet." Four days later, Henry Lamb, who runs a group devoted to world-government fears called Sovereignty International, penned a column on World Net Daily starting with the words "Hooray for Glenn Beck! Right out there in front of God and everybody, he talks about global governance as a real and present danger." Lamb went on to cite a 1997 quotation from the head of the World Resources Institute and a 1976 report by the United Nations Conference on Human Settlements.

Three days after Lamb's column, Beck was back on the air, proclaiming that "we are headed towards global governance." Without mentioning Lamb or World Net Daily, Beck's monologue included the very same 1976 and 1997 quotations from Lamb's column.

Still, the global-governance panic was but a faint echo of the FEMA concentration camp hysteria.

On March 26, 2009, more than three weeks after setting the conspiracy world on fire with this "can't debunk" claim, Beck was back on the air with the story. "America, we have a real problem in this country," he said. "We don't know what the truth is anymore."

Now, why might that be?

He said he asked his guest, James Meigs from *Popular Mechanics*, to investigate the FEMA thing. And Meigs said, "It looks, from our early reporting, like a classic conspiracy theory." That still wasn't enough, and Beck said he'd have Meigs back in a couple of weeks.

He made good on his promise, and on April 6, Meigs reported that the buildings in Wyoming that were supposed to be part of the alleged concentration camps had either been boarded up, knocked down, or were being used to repair trains.

"Well, Auschwitz had trains," Beck said. "I'm just saying."

"But once you go down that road, if somebody wants to be convinced of that, they can't really debunk that," Meigs pointed out. He also noted that the woman who had narrated the Internet video purporting to show a FEMA concentration camp with gas chambers was a militia movement leader who recommended that her followers "march on Washington and start executing senators."

These are the people Beck had given a national television audience.

"One last question," he said. "Take a look at this picture . . . Is this what they claim? This is a concentration camp?"

"Yes, it is," Meigs answered.

"Are there atrocities going on in that camp?"

"There is every reason to believe there is," Meigs answered.

"Is this a government-run concentration camp where atrocities—every reason to believe atrocities are going on?"

"Yes."

Beck left this story hanging until the next day's show, when he finally let Meigs say that the concentration camp in the photo was located . . . in North Korea. Meigs said somebody used the photo, from a human rights group's report, "slapped the Department of Homeland Security logo on it and claimed that these are on American soil."

And that Photoshop expert was elevated by Beck to a national newsmaker, as the Fox News host hinted and implied for more than a month that the Obama administration was operating a concentration camp for political dissidents.

Weeks later, Fox's O'Reilly asked Beck about a column by Paul Krugman in the *New York Times* saying Beck "warned viewers the Federal Emergency Management Agency might be building concentration camps as part of the Obama administration's totalitarian agenda."

"I never said that," Beck replied.

No, he said that his research "can't debunk" the concentration camps and, in the next breath, advised those viewers who "fear that we might be heading towards a totalitarian state: Look out. Buckle up. There's something going on in our country that is—ain't good."

No doubt many Beck viewers missed his carefully crafted reversal and still believe today that Obama operates his own Auschwitz for political opponents.

CHAPTER 13
THE FACTS ARE STUBBORN THINGS

* *

"There are so many loosey-goosey facts here on today's show," Glenn Beck told his Fox viewers one evening early in 2010. What he was saying was true. The question is why he felt the need to make the disclosure on that particular show, when it could be applied equally to just about every one of his shows.

There are lies, there are damn lies, and there is *The Glenn Beck Show*. Sometimes he posits falsehoods of no great import. Sometimes they are falsehoods that completely turn reality on its head. More often, Beck begins with a kernel of truth and then bakes the kernel in a casserole of bizarre suppositions. He then serves up a wildly implausible prediction—which by definition can't be disproved because it has not yet happened. There is no way to prove that the country will *not* be taken over by fascists next year, any more than it is possible to prove that the earth will not be destroyed by an asteroid next year.

Beck's frequent history lessons are steeped in "facts." Such as this fact that he produced on *Fox & Friends* one morning in the form of a question about the untapped oil in Alaska: "Why did we buy Alaska in the 1950s?" A good question—particularly since Alaska was purchased in 1867.

"We have the Age of Enlightenment, 1620 to 1871, uh, 1781," Beck said in another history lesson. "This was a time when people said, wait a minute, wait a minute, we can think out of the box. This is coming out of the Dark Ages." The Dark Ages ended in about 1000 AD, but what's an extra six hundred years here or there?

Beck used history again to liken the Obama administration to imperial Russia, by discussing his use of "czars"— powerful advisers who are not confirmed by the Senate. "We're talking about these thirty-two czars" in the Obama administration, he said. "But we really don't even know who these czars are because they don't answer to the Congress. They don't have to be approved by the Congress . . . What are we doing?"

What we are doing is making stuff up as we go along. Turns out, according to the University of Pennsylvania–affiliated FactCheck.org, nine of the thirty-two were confirmed by the Senate, eight were not appointed by the president, and another seven were in positions created by past administrations. FactCheck further found out that George W. Bush's administration had been even more "czar-ist" with thirty-five.

Historian Beck presented to his viewers the news that "Thomas Jefferson created the Marines for the Islamic pirates that were happening, right?" Sorry, not right. The Marines, as the group PolitiFact points out, were created in 1775, then reactivated in 1798 under President John Adams to deal with French, not Islamic, pirates. Beck, however, has his own texts offering their own facts. Recommending a book one night by a conservative who rewrote the history of the nation's founding, Beck asserted that the book must be true because "it's all footnoted." Modern history is also problematic for Beck. He said of Obama: "This guy is dangerous. He's never lost before. He won't understand it." Obama lost a congressional primary in 2000. Beck said his "best bud," economist and columnist Paul Krugman, "missed the industry's $8 trillion housing bubble." Alas for Beck, a Nexis search finds that Krugman warned as early as 2002 in his column that "more and more people are using the B-word about the housing market."

"History has proven over and over again," distinguished professor of history Beck lectured at another point, "that government is not the answer." Obama did not understand this lesson, the professor continued, because he has so few people in his cabinet with "private sector experience"—

"under 10 percent" for Obama, compared to "over 50 percent" for Nixon. Beck was basing this view on an article on Forbes.com that turned out to be wrong. The correct number for Obama was more like a third—higher if you look at all cabinet-level appointees.

Numbers can be problematic for a man with a point to make. Beck got tripped up by these infernal digits when he informed his audience that 49 percent of Americans "don't pay any tax." Actually, fewer than 10 percent pay no federal taxes, and even fewer pay no state taxes; the 49 percent were those who don't pay federal income taxes.

Likewise, Beck delivered the alarming news that Chile was ranked third in the world in "economic freedom," and the United States was seventeenth in the same study. Scary—if true. PolitiFact, an offshoot of the *St. Petersburg Times*, located the source of Beck's figures: the conservative CATO Institute, which actually put Chile in fifth place, and the United States a fraction of a point behind, in sixth.

Maybe that was just a misunderstanding. Numbers can be so confusing. But it's hard to say the same of Beck's assertion on his radio show that "in the health-care bill, we're now offering insurance for dogs." There was nothing of the sort in the bill.

And what to make of Beck's assertion on his Fox News show that the United States is "the only country in the world" that grants automatic citizenship to those born here. Turns out, as PolitiFact pointed out, there are thirty-four such countries, so Beck was off—let's see here—by thirty-three.

Many of these discrepancies are of little consequence. But sometimes Beck will sneak in a whopper that fundamentally revises the historical record. Consider his claim of April 2009 that Obama, "when confronted with the spending and socialism bailouts . . . has reminded us over and over again that President Bush was in office when [the] TARP bailout happened. Well, we were all against that!"

We were? Then how do we explain this Beck quotation from September 2008, a mere seven months earlier? "It takes everything in me to say this," he said then, but "I think the bailout is the right thing to do. The real story is the $700 billion that you're hearing about now[, which] is not only, I believe, necessary, it is also not nearly enough, and all of the weasels in Washington know it."

But Beck, though a newcomer to government spending restraint, still was not going to be moved away from his criticism of Obama's spending. On one show, he claimed that "the highest" level of spending under Franklin D. Roosevelt was 12 percent of GDP, in 1941. "This is what Obama is planning on spending," he went on. "Whoa! Remember—highest, 1941, was 12 percent. Here's the lowest [for Obama, in 2013] at 22.8 percent."

But Beck left out a few relevant numbers, such as FDR's spending in 1942 (24.3 percent), 1943 (43.6 percent), 1944 (43.6 percent), and 1945 (41.9 percent).

The loosey-goosey nature of Beck's facts might be easier to dismiss as entertainment if so many didn't take Beck's claims at face value—even those who should know better, such as members of Congress.

On June 21, 2010, in one of his "Crime Inc." installments, Beck went after the liberal billionaire George Soros, whom he described as a currency manipulator of Jewish ancestry with "disturbing hair in his nose."

Beck told his viewers that the Obama administration made "a $2 billion preliminary commitment for Petrobras"—the Brazilian oil company—"just days after he [Soros] strengthened his investment" in the company. "Then Obama suspends the deepwater drilling at 1,500 meters," Beck went on. "Petrobras is drilling at 2,777 meters. Obama knows it and loans $2 billion to Petrobras."

This allegation, reported by Beck as fact, turned out to be an Internet rumor that had been disproved nine months earlier by FactCheck. The "preliminary commitment" to Petrobras was not from the Obama administration but from the U.S. Export-Import Bank—at a time when all five members of the bank's board had been appointed by George W. Bush. The loan from the bank, which is self-funded and doesn't rely on taxpayer money, was to buy U.S.-made oil-field equipment. And Soros actually reduced his stake in Petrobras before any of the loan had been made.

But Beck's version of the "facts" was good enough for Rep. Dan Burton, a veteran Indiana Republican. "The thing that really is funny about this is we just sent $2 billion to Brazil so they could do offshore drilling," he said on the House floor the day after Beck's report on the topic. "We don't need to be sending Mr. Soros money in Brazil so he can make more money by doing offshore drilling with our taxpayers' money."

At least Burton didn't mention Soros's Jewish ancestry and his nose hair.

Facts can be such messy things. That's why it's better to clean them up a little before taking them out in public—or, better yet, leaving the messiest ones at home.

On the third day of Supreme Court nominee Elena Kagan's confirmation hearings before the Senate, for example, Beck said that Kagan had "strongly implied" in an argument before the Supreme Court that political books could be censored. "You know, that doesn't make me feel warm and fuzzy inside that we got a person that would sit on the Supreme Court and say 'ban books.' Get the hell out of my courtroom!"

What Beck neglected to mention was that Kagan, in testimony the day before, explained that her job in making the argument as U.S. Solicitor General was "to defend the statute as it was written" and not to offer her own opinion. Kagan told the committee that "the act ought not to be applied" to books, that "we thought it never would be applied to books," and that "to the extent that anybody ever tries to apply it to books, what I argued in the court was that there would be a good constitutional challenge to that."

Long before Beck accused Kagan of a book-banning crusade, he asserted that union leader Andy Stern was "the most frequent visitor of the White House, over the secretary of state and everybody else."

But White House visitor logs released a week before Beck made that charge showed that the most frequent visitor at the White House up to that point was Treasury adviser Lee Sachs, whose ninety-two visits were nearly quadruple Stern's twenty-four. And it turned out the secretary of state's visits weren't captured in the visitor log because she doesn't have to go through the regular Secret Service security gate. But this wasn't nearly as sexy as Beck's claim about Stern being "the most frequent," which may have had something to do with his basing his report on an earlier, incomplete release of visitor data.

Likewise, a crucial detail was obscured when Beck delivered his alarming report that those who logged on to the "cash for clunkers" program at CARS.gov could have their computers' contents "seized" by the feds.

"You log on to this at your home, everything in your home is now theirs?" Beck asked his guest.

"Basically," she replied.

"Good God Almighty!" Beck said.

That *did* sound pretty bad. Except that, on further review, it turned out this only applied to car dealers, not car owners, and even dealers wouldn't have to surrender their private information to the government. "I'm sorry, I'm sorry," Beck said with mock regret on a later show after this was pointed out to him.

When somebody says things that aren't true, he's not necessarily a liar; he may just be uninformed. In Beck's case, however, this possibility was tested and discarded by no less an authority than the ladies of *The View* on ABC. Beck appeared on the show one morning and was immediately ambushed by Whoopi Goldberg and Barbara Walters over a description he'd given on the radio of a recent meeting among the three of them on an Amtrak train bound for Washington.

Beck claimed that the women approached him on the train to talk, and that Goldberg and Walters had "reserved" seats on the train, contrary to Amtrak's policy of not assigning seats—and then he had a good laugh with his listeners. Turns out neither claim was true.

Confronted on live television, Beck immediately confessed to "a mischaracterization" of the circumstances of their meeting. "Why did you lie about that?" asked Joy Behar.

"I don't know," was Beck's response.

"You just had a brain fart or what?" Behar pressed.

"You're accusing me of lying," Beck countercharged, recovering.

"You did lie," Goldberg said. "You're a lying sack of dog mess."

Beck finally apologized. "I'm sorry that I, to use Nancy Pelosi's words, misspoke."

Walters, informing Beck that she had not reserved a seat, wanted to know why he claimed otherwise. "You are an investigative reporter," she said.

"No, I'm not," Beck said.

"You're a reporter."

"No, I'm not."

"So you check no facts at all?" Walters asked.

"No," Beck answered. "No. I am a commentator."

And being a commentator means never having to say you're wrong.

The most frightening Beck assertions, though, are not about botched facts or numbers. They are assertions that would strike an ordinary person as zany—but just might be believed by a small minority, such as three million nightly Beck viewers. American liberals, he asserts, "have been raised to hate the United States government in many ways."

Union supporters "are also for one world government." How to disprove this? Polygraphs?

Likewise, when black Democratic congressmen claimed that hecklers on Capitol Hill shouted epithets and spit on them, Beck went on air to say there's "no proof or evidence of any spitting." Perhaps he expected a saliva sample to be provided.

But if Beck's more outlandish accusations and theories cannot be "proven" with things such as "facts," they can be documented lavishly. That's where the chalkboard comes in.

On a typical night, it contains the word "Radical?" in one corner, then the word "Obama" in big letters. Then, as if illustrating a complex scientific reaction, it has arrows pointing every which way, but all of them ultimately leading to Obama. The mad assortment of arrows goes back and forth among Beck's usual suspects, "Communist Party," "ACORN," "Apollo Alliance," and "Van Jones."

"We have Rashid Khalidi, who is—who is a radical in his own right, tied directly to Barack Obama," Beck will narrate, explaining the chaotic diagram. "Carl Davidson is connected to the New Party, which is connected to the Movement for Democratic Society, to progressives, to Van Jones, to Jeff Jones—it's all connected!"

And it's true: They *are* connected—by chalk arrows. But in Beck's description, this is proof that the government is run by communists. "The radicals are all down here," scientist Beck explains. "They start to filter up and they come to places like the Apollo Alliance and they filter up, and they're scrubbed clean, so they don't look like radicals anymore—but they're all tied here."

Arrows are a uniquely effective weapon in Beck's quiver. He proved that Supreme Court justice Sonia Sotomayor was connected to ACORN by drawing an arrow from "Sotomayor," through the Capitol dome, to the ACORN logo.

And if arrows are not available, a juxtaposition of photographs is sufficient to prove connection and causality—as when Obama aide Valerie Jarrett was tied to Che Guevara. Another night, Beck put the phrase "Six Degrees of Obama" on the chalkboard. By moving photographs around, Beck was able to prove that Obama was tied to Chairman Mao, Venezuela's Chávez, and other nasties.

"This is my theory. You can call and correct it," he offered, over the air, to the White House. No call came in—so the theory must be accurate.

Same thing with Beck's theory that the government was preparing to confiscate Americans' land to pay off the federal debt. "Conjecture on my part," he began—so it must be true! "How about we just print enough money to pay off the debt over time. Sure, I mean, it will be worthless, but we'll be able to honor our agreement." And how to keep the currency from collapsing? "There's certainly enough land

and resources in America that we could back our currency with. I mean, the government—the government, though, would have to own all of the land," Beck explained. "Oh, my gosh, I just thought of something: Between Fannie and Freddie, the government already owns half of all of some of the U.S. mortgages and they're about to buy more."

So the federal government, through Fannie Mae and Freddie Mac, was about to sell Americans' homes and property to the Chinese? "Look, America, I'm hoping that I'm wrong about this. But I can't figure out anything else."

Proof positive!

The conspiracy extends to every government action. ACORN designed government-run health care. The Apollo Alliance wrote the stimulus legislation. The Service Employees International Union is drafting immigration laws and consulting on Afghanistan strategy. On rare occasions there is a glimmer of self-awareness, as Beck mocks his own conspiracy talk; one night, while tying ACORN to every possible malefactor, he jokingly included a mug shot of the evil Silas, from *The Da Vinci Code*.

"Tonight," Beck said one evening, "I want to talk to you about something that somebody said earlier to me today: 'You know, Glenn, don't you think you're going to go into loopy territory?' No, I think the world is moving into the loopy territory. I'm just trying to explain what's happening."

One of Beck's cleverest ways to float a good conspiracy theory without fear of facts getting in the way is to say he is "not saying" that which he is saying. For example:

"I'm not saying that Obama has an enemies list, but I wouldn't put it past him, either."

"I'm not saying that we have a bunch of mullahs or some star chamber running the country."

"I'm not saying that we're like Russia. I'm not saying Obama is going to kill anybody."

"I'm not saying being poor in America is sweet."

"I'm not saying to shoot anybody."

He's just saying.

After the Fort Hood army base shooting, Beck said this was an Al-Qaeda "shark bump" presaging a bigger attack: "I'm not saying this was a coordinated shark bump, but this is a shark bump."

One night, he alarmed his audience with a Muslim apocalyptic theory about a man who is "supposed to create a global government" and who tells Christians to "submit or he cuts their heads off." Added Beck: "I'm not saying these things are true."

Rallying his audience to dig up dirt on the ACORN community organization, he said: "I'm not saying there is anything nefarious here, I think there is. It smells—it smells pretty rotten here."

Another time, he warned that the new "smart grid"

electricity system could be used by the government to take "critical information out of your house." Then came the usual disclaimer: "I'm not saying that Obama or the Democrats or the Republicans or anybody are going to take this technology and use it this way. However, you know . . . Who knows what could happen?"

Who knows? But, in Beck's world, knowing is not a prerequisite to broadcasting.

This has caused some concern among Beck's colleagues at Fox. Privately, many producers and correspondents at the cable network talk about their concerns that working on Beck's broadcast will tarnish their reputations as journalists. *Washington Post* media critic Howie Kurtz reported on a "deep split" within Fox, where "many journalists are worried about the prospect that Beck is becoming the face of the network." Fox boss Roger Ailes, though a Beck booster, "has occasionally spoken to Beck about the negative tone" of his show, Kurtz reported.

★ ★ ★

The relatively straight-shooting Fox anchor Shepard Smith once previewed Beck's hour by telling viewers that "Glenn Beck will be live with us from his Fear Chamber." Beck later said he preferred the term "Doom Room."

Beck, in turn, uses Fox News as a truth shield. "Who owns this network? Rupert Murdoch," he reminded viewers in April 2010. "Do you think he's going to let a guy at five o'clock say a bunch of stuff, put this together, it's completely wrong, and stay on the network? . . . Because Fox couldn't allow me to say things that were wrong."

Or could it? Bill O'Reilly, the prime-time Fox star who holds himself to a stricter factual diet than Beck, once interviewed Beck on his 8 P.M. show about his incendiary style.

"I don't know why I'm successful," Beck said in the interview.

"I don't either, to tell you the truth," O'Reilly said. "But you take it five steps further than I do."

Might have something to do with it. One night in May 2010, Beck, in an off-camera performance for a live audience, offered a rare confession as he joked about how something "just came out of my mouth during my monologue on TV." Oops—just popped right out. "Sometimes they come out of my mouth and I'm like, 'Whoa! Wow. Where did that come from?' "

Many have asked the same question.

CHAPTER 14

A KINDRED SOUL

* *

It was the sort of stem-winder viewers of the Glenn Beck show are accustomed to hearing each night.

It had hints of doom: "Tuesday of this week—Tuesday, January 29th—will be remembered by our offspring as the day which overshadowed July 4th. The one date was associated with our independence. The other with our stupid betrayal."

It had fear of foreigners: "On Tuesday of this week the United States Senate is about to hand over our national sovereignty . . . Without sovereignty a nation is but a shadow. With sovereignty it is a substance capable of existing in peace and security, in law and order, free from the dictates of external powers."

It questioned the patriotism of his opponents: "There has arisen in our midst a false philosophy which looks askance upon nationalism and disparages the realities of life . . . It prefers to sing the praise of the yellow peril of pacifism while it berates and belittles the vigorous valor of patriotism. It subscribes to the utopian dreams of world peace."

It claimed the support of the Founding Fathers: "I appeal to them by the blood spilled at Valley Forge, by the fatherly admonitions of Washington and Jefferson which still ring in our ears, not to jeopardize our freedom, not to barter our sovereignty, not to entangle us with the religious, the racial, the economic, and the martial affairs of the Old World."

It had a note of martyrdom: "Perhaps I am out of tune with the tempo of modern events in giving expression to my fears and to my patriotism . . . I am on the losing side and I am subjecting myself to ridicule, to ignominy, and perhaps to chastisement. But cost what it may, the American people have a right to know the unvarnished truth of facts."

It hinted at violence: "Perhaps that is something for the Senators to think about as innocently they tie the Gordian knot . . . around the throat of the American public. It is easy to tie but perhaps it can be severed only by a sword. By a sword, say I? Most certainly!"

It had jingoistic notes: "I appeal to every solid American who loves democracy, who loves the United States, who loves the truth, to . . . fight to keep America safe for Americans."

And, naturally, it all came down to godless communism:

"I am opposed to communism as much as I am opposed to a plague . . . In years to come when you young men and young women who are listening to me this afternoon will have had your economic lives melted down to the standards of England, of France, of Spain, and of Mexico, when you will be marshaled into an army to fight the red ruin of communism, I pray that you will still have faith in the brotherhood of man as preached by Christ."

In fact, the only atypical thing about this rant was that it was uttered in 1935, twenty-nine years before Beck was born. These were the words of the Reverend Charles E. Coughlin, "Father Coughlin," the populist radio priest of the Great Depression whose denunciations of Franklin Roosevelt attracted millions.

Coughlin flamed out after embracing fascism before the Second World War. Lately, however, the ghost of Coughlin has been seen and heard often on the airwaves. Chris Matthews was doing a show on the latest outrage by Beck in late 2009 when the specter visited the set.

"What we're seeing now is what we've seen before in American history," David Brooks, the conservative *New York Times* columnist said of the "race-baiting" techniques of Beck and Rush Limbaugh. "What we're seeing: Father Coughlin," Brooks said. "That's what these guys are . . . They are taking over the Republican Party. And so if the Republican Party is sane, they will say no to these people.

But every single elected leader in the Republican Party is afraid to take on Rush and Glenn Beck."

The accusation was evidently confounding to Beck, because, by his own admission, he had to figure out just who Father Coughlin was. A few months later, he went on air to report the result of his studies.

"The left loves to call me Father Coughlin," he said, although Brooks, at least, resides on the reasonable right. "That's a real insult. It is—especially now that I've done my research and I know who this man is.

"I'm called many things by the left, because of my viewpoints, but the only thing that they really love to trot out over and over again is that I'm Father Coughlin," Beck continued. "You'll see that it's laughable. It's a deep insult to be compared to him. But it's hysterical because it's such—it's so ridiculously inaccurate. It doesn't even make sense."

Beck laid out his defense: "Yes, Father Coughlin was against communism. Yes, he was on the radio like me. Yes, he was against the sitting president, FDR. But it's weird, because that's where it ends—because he was initially a supporter of FDR. He was also wildly anti-Semitic. Not me. He was for big unions. You know how much I love the unions . . . He's also for social justice, the union man. Yes. That's me in a nutshell, isn't it?"

More than he'd like to admit.

Coughlin, a small-town priest in Michigan with an Irish brogue, reached 10 million people with his radio broadcasts on an average Sunday and as many as 40 million on some. He was perhaps the most powerful voice for populism and isolationism in the 1930s, at least until he became increasingly anti-Semitic ("when we get through with the Jews in America, they'll think the treatment they received in Germany was nothing") and associated himself with a violent anticommunist group. The Vatican ordered him silent and radio stations refused to carry his shows.

But before he self-destructed, Coughlin had some things to say that would sound very familiar to viewers of the 5 P.M. hour on Fox News.

Beck on the Fed: "The Federal Reserve is made up of a bunch of unelected bankers. They determine the country's monetary policy and hold the future of this country right in their hands. Now, people across the country are crawling for transparency in the Fed. A lot of people are saying, 'Why don't we abolish the Fed?' "

Coughlin on the Fed: "If we are lovers of the principle of America for the Americans, we will drive out the international bankers from their stronghold of Federal bank ownership . . . The Federal Reserve banking system was the conveyor of destruction. Instead of rescuing finance from the hands of politicians, it betrayed it into the bondage of financial overlords."

Beck on Woodrow Wilson: "Woodrow Wilson ran for

re-election and he just barely won. And he said we're never going to go to war in Europe. Lo and behold, just a few months later, World War I!"

Coughlin on Woodrow Wilson: "Although elected to his high office on the promise of keeping us out of the war, he now submitted to the fallacy that it was more sacred to protect the capitalistic dollar than to preserve the life of a mother's son!"

Beck on revolution: "My question tonight is: When do we ever run those who are bankrupting our country and literally stealing our children's future out of town? Grab a torch."

Coughlin on revolution: "I would ask the industrialists whether or not they and their children could logically anticipate a time in the not distant future when they will become targets for the wrath of a despoiled people."

Beck on communists in the White House: The president "may be a full-fledged Marxist. He has surrounded himself by Marxists his whole life . . . His friends, his nominees and everything, they're all Marxist."

Coughlin on communists in the White House: The president "shares the responsibility of having endorsed a most radical leaning towards international socialism or Sovietism."

Beck on being above partisan politics: "Stop looking at it through the partisan lens. Both parties are screwing you. Ignore the R or D next to their name."

Coughlin on being above partisan politics: "The Democratic and Republican parties . . . are one, the left wing and the other right wing of the same bird of prey."

Coughlin tended toward the dramatic oratory of his day; Beck speaks in the casual and conversational style of his. But they both were brilliant and captivating performers. "Coughlin," writes Alan Brinkley in his book about Coughlin and Huey Long, *Voices of Protest*, "used a wide variety of rhetorical techniques: maudlin sentimentality, anger and invective, sober reasonableness, religious or patriotic fervor . . . in this unpredictability lay much of Coughlin's appeal."

Beck, likewise, is alternately funny and apocalyptic, reasonable and incendiary. Even his public weeping has a Coughlin-like precedent. With tears on his cheeks, Coughlin told a crowd in 1936: "President Roosevelt can be a dictator if he wants to."

Beck has inherited the "dictator" meme from his radio predecessor; in one radio segment, he accused President Obama of following in the path of "many brutal dictators."

In fairness, Beck is probably not imitating Coughlin. He's drawing from the same strain in American politics that can be traced back to the beginning of the republic. There has always been a tension between urban elites and the rural masses, and the latter group has long had an innate fear of collusion between the government and the wealthy. This was what Richard Hofstadter described in his classic 1960s study "The Paranoid Style in American Politics."

American political life, he wrote, "has served again and again as an arena for uncommonly angry minds . . . Behind such movements there is a style of mind, not always right-wing in its affiliations, that has a long and varied history. I call it the paranoid style simply because no other word adequately evokes the qualities of heated exaggeration, suspiciousness, and conspiratorial fantasy that I have in mind."

Hofstadter saw this style in the anti-Masonic movement of the 1820s, the Populist Party of the 1890s, and the McCarthy era of the 1950s. "In the 1930s, the chief vehicle of right-wing discontent was Father Coughlin's Social Justice movement, a depression phenomenon drawing the bulk of its support from those who suffered most from bad times—the working class and the unemployed, farmers and some of the lower middle class," he wrote. "It played on old Populist themes, attacked international bankers, demanded free silver and other changes in the money and credit system, and resorted to an anti-Semitic rhetoric far more virulent than anything the Populists would have dreamed of."

Times change, but the demagogue's tools are forever.

He must, for example, warn his followers of imminent takeover by foreigners. In Coughlin's day, it was an attempt by the Roosevelt administration to join the World Court, part of the League of Nations. "Our entrance into this flag-less nation," he said, "belittles the vigorous valor of patri-otism."

Beck, updating the technique, fights international agree-ments on climate and anything else the United Nations tries to do. "I will vehemently oppose any measure giving another country, the United Nations, or any other entity power over U.S. citizens," he said.

The successful demagogue must also hint darkly of vio-lence to come. Coughlin had visions of "a revolution in this country which will make the French Revolution look silly." He said his ideas "must be fought for unto death, if neces-sary."

Beck, taking Coughlin's baton, warns of "something far worse than the Depression," something like a "possible uprising here in the United States." He outlined a scenario of "something that maybe we have never even seen before, including the Civil War."

The would-be leader of the angry masses must also ready his ranks for martyrdom. "You can prepare yourself for reprisals," Coughlin warned his millions of listeners. "You will be referred to as nit-wits and morons. Your pro-gram will be disparaged as the brain-child of a demagogic crackpot and your organization will be listed among the so-called radicals . . . If patriotism is referred to as bigoted isolation, we will gladly accept these charges with the same philosophic attitude in which our forebears were trade-marked with the name of rebel and revolutionist."

Beck's modern version: "People will again be afraid, be afraid this time of being called a racist or a bigot or a hate-monger. America, you speak without fear, or . . . you will not be able to speak, and you will experience the kind of fear that no one in this country has experienced before. All it will take—God help us all—all it will take is an event, or an emergency."

In philosophy, there is one big difference between the two men. Coughlin spoke weekly of "social justice"—making sure the workingman got a share of the capitalist's fortune—and formed the National Union for Social Justice. The antitax Beck, a rich man's Coughlin, uses the same term, "social justice," but has determined that it is at the root of communism, fascism, dictatorship, and every other evil short of tooth decay.

Yet even here, their styles are similar: Each man claims that God supports his interpretation of social justice. Coughlin waved around Pope Pius XI's encyclical stating that government should "adjust ownership to meet the needs of the public good." Beck, in turn, instructed listeners: "Look for the words 'social justice' or 'economic justice' on your church Web site. If you find them, run as fast as you can."

Beck, based on his research on Coughlin, told viewers

that his predecessor "perverted American ideals for his own power and most importantly for social justice." The radio priest, Beck argued, "thought FDR's policies didn't go far enough." Further, Beck concluded that Coughlin was the "spookiest dude you've ever seen" and very different from his own movement. "You wouldn't have this at the Tea Party," Beck said of Coughlin's fascist turn. "Tea parties are for small, limited government."

Beck, in his research, may have missed this central part of Coughlin's philosophy: "I believe in the simplification of government and the further lifting of crushing taxation from the slender revenues of the laboring class." Or that bit about Coughlin being "wholly opposed to the Roosevelt taxes." Or when Coughlin accused FDR of running up "the greatest debt in all history."

And Beck at times sounds much like Coughlin as he gives a populist denunciation of government help for big business. "You have the global politicians, worldwide businessmen, and international bankers all trying to protect and stabilize giant global corporations," he laments, "because their money and their influence helps the politicians grab even more power in their home countries."

It's true that Beck's message, seventy-five years after Coughlin, has changed to reflect the times. But the imagery has changed little:

Americans in chains. Coughlin fought "the modern

industrial slavery" and the "slavery of modern mass production." Beck says Obama is "moving all of us quickly in slavery" and warns against becoming "a slave to what's being built in Washington."

Government sliding into tyranny. Coughlin said Roosevelt was "usurping federal power," becoming a "financial dictator," and warned of the "present despotism, which is far more acute than was taxation without representation." Beck likens Obama administration officials to earlier "tyrants" and "slave owners."

Guardian of the Constitution. Coughlin saw himself as defender of the nation's founding document; "the day has arrived when we must expel those who have forgotten our Constitution," he said. Beck sees his political opposition as "the cancer in America and it is eating our Constitution, and it was designed to eat the Constitution."

Fear of Europe. Coughlin warned of a U.S. government trying to force its people "down to the European standard of living, now that we are determined to accept the European standard of diplomacy and in part at least the European standard of legislation." Beck sees America "marching down the road to European socialized health care."

Both men positioned themselves as leader of a movement rather than a mere broadcaster: Coughlin formed the National Union for Social Justice to shape laws and elections; Beck created the 9/12 Project to do the same. Both men claimed the Founding Fathers would support their views. Both favored alternatives to currency—silver for Coughlin, gold for Beck. Both had their demons—Coughlin's "Bourbons" and "money changers," and Beck's "progressives."

And both proudly took sides in the battle between God and communism: "The apostles of Lenin and Trotsky bid us forsake all rights to private ownership and . . . [summon] us to worship at the altar where a dictator of flesh and blood is enthroned as our god and the citizens are branded as his slaves."

Communists, dictators, and slaves: Vintage Beck. Except that last quote was from Coughlin.

CHAPTER 15

SOME OF HIS BEST FRIENDS . . .

· ·

You can take the man out of the *Morning Zoo*, but you can't take the *Morning Zoo* out of the man.

It's been years since Beck has done a drive-time radio show, but he still saves some of his best material for the morning. It was on *Fox & Friends*, the Fox News morning show, that he said he just couldn't prove that the federal government wasn't operating a Nazi-style concentration camp in Wyoming. And it was on that same show almost five months later that he uttered the words that would come to define him.

One of the hosts, Steve Doocy, reminded viewers that the White House was about to have a "beer fest" in which Obama would bring together the black Harvard professor Henry Louis Gates Jr. and the white Cambridge cop who arrested him while he was breaking into his own home.

Obama, after too hastily scolding the cops for being "stupid," wanted to have a "teachable moment" on race.

"That is unbelievable," Beck said of the planned beer summit.

"Why?"

"That is unbelievable," the incredulous Beck repeated. Waving his index finger, he continued: "Why? For a teaching lesson? Some sort of a—who needs to learn what here? This person I think has exposed himself as a guy, over and over and over again, who has a deep-seated hatred for white people or the white culture, I don't know what it is."

But Beck did know this: "You can't sit in a pew with Jeremiah Wright for twenty years and not hear some of that stuff and not have it wash over. What kind of President of the United States immediately jumps on the police? . . . Now they're going to have a beer? That's obscene."

Gretchen Carlson, another host, tried to change the subject to whether or not Obama had planned what he was going to say about the incident when asked about it at a news conference.

But Beck was not going to be taken off his theme. He said it didn't matter if it was "off the cuff or planned. This guy has a social justice—he is going to set all of the wrongs of past right."

"But listen," the third host, Brian Kilmeade, interjected. "You can't say he doesn't like white people. David Axelrod is white, Rahm Emanuel his chief of staff is white, I think 70 percent of the people we see every day are white. Robert Gibbs is white."

Beck only now appeared to be realizing that he had just said something explosive. "I'm not saying he doesn't like white people," he replied, having just said exactly that. "I'm saying he has a problem. He has a—this guy is, I believe, a racist."

So much for qualifying his accusation. Beck, sitting cross-legged in the guest chair, continued on, ranting about an Obama adviser who believes in "black liberation theology. A black nationalist." He emphasized the word "black."

The reaction was instantaneous, and unflattering. "ARE YOU SERIOUS????" MSNBC's morning host, former Republican congressman Joe Scarborough, tweeted. "Did Glenn Beck really say the president has 'a deep-seated hatred for white people or the white culture'? Outrageous."

Even Fox executives felt the need to say that Beck wasn't speaking for the network.

★ ★ ★

Beck played the race game when he was on the *Morning Zoo* (he memorably mocked an Asian American accent), but it became more of a problem as he gained followers.

During one of his radio broadcasts in 2007, Beck observed of rising Democratic star Barack Obama: "He's very white in many ways . . . Can I even say that without somebody else starting a campaign saying 'what does he mean he's very white.' He is. He's very white."

But that was a racist thing to say—according to Glenn Beck. That same year he scolded Jesse Jackson: "He says Barack Obama is acting white, which is an unbelievable racist statement."

The previous year, he had Keith Ellison, the first Muslim elected to Congress, as a guest on his CNN program. "You are a Democrat," he told the congressman. "You are saying, 'let's cut and run.' And I have to tell you, I have been nervous about this interview with you, because what I feel like saying is, 'Sir, prove to me that you are not working with our enemies.'"

Added Beck: "And I know you're not. I'm not accusing you of being an enemy, but that's the way I feel, and I think a lot of Americans will feel that way."

"I don't need to prove my patriotic stripes," the congressman replied.

After Obama was elected, Beck, on his radio show, determined that Americans elected him because of his color. They "were voting for, uh, you know, not change, but change I think in race . . . They weren't necessarily for his policies."

"People said, 'at least he's not another old white guy,'" chimed in his executive producer.

Though Beck bristles at the idea that such remarks might earn him the "racist" label, he's often happy to bestow the distinction on others.

Sonia Sotomayor, a Hispanic woman nominated by Obama to the Supreme Court, uttered "one of the most outrageous racist remarks I have heard," Beck articulated one night.

Reading her oft-criticized remark that "a wise Latina woman . . . would more often than not reach a better conclusion than a white male," Beck commented, "Gosh, that smacks of racism, but maybe it's just me."

Beck's guest, conservative legal scholar Ed Whelan, dutifully assured the host that it wasn't just him.

"I don't like the charges of, 'oh, you're a racist,'" Beck continued. Unless he's the one leveling the charge. "I mean, gee. She sure sounds like a racist here," he added.

And given that the president and his Supreme Court justice are racists, it's only natural that the nation should reintroduce slavery. He mentioned slavery and slaves some two hundred times in his first year on Fox News:

"I think this president is moving quickly, moving all of us quickly, into slavery. He's enslaving our children with a debt that they just can never repay."

"We are enslaved now to China, we're at China's whim."

"Don't allow yourself to become, or your state to become, a slave to what's being built in Washington."

"Progressive policies are keeping these people in slavery—slavery to government, welfare, affirmative action, regulation, control."

"We have new slaves, illegal immigrants, being used the same by the same people, although conditions are not as bad as they were, but it's the same damn argument."

"Rebuking Joe Wilson doesn't help solve any real race problems or any problems with anything, including the existing slavery that we have with illegal immigration and ACORN."

"They'll sell you and your children into slavery in order to do special favors for their cronies."

"This isn't a Tree of Liberty anymore. This is slavery. This is slavery."

How to make sense of all this racism and enslavement? Beck called in Jesse Lee Peterson, a black conservative. "I have to tell you, Glenn, the electing of Barack Obama was about black racism and white guilt," the minister explained. "White Americans want to make up for past history, slavery, and they have been blamed for what is happening today."

White people, he reasoned, "think by electing a black socialist liberal, somehow or another, black Americans are going to overcome their racism. But the only thing that is going to change their racism is black folks have to forgive. They have to drop their anger."

Beck's racial anger, however, was under no such restriction. Not only did he regard Obama as a racist, he regarded

Obama as a racist with a bladder problem. When Obama declined to meet with the CEO of BP, the oil company that caused the Gulf of Mexico oil spill, Beck speculated that the snub was because the oil man "is a white CEO." Around that same time Beck said he was dismayed at Obama's inclination "to pee all over our allies," and asserted that "the only thing this president hasn't done is just urinate on us."

The census, which asks Americans to identify themselves by race, caused an eruption in Beck's racial volcano. "Why are they asking this question today?" he asked on his radio show.

"Because minorities are worth more than whites," replied his producer.

"Exactly right," Beck informed his listeners. "So you will get more dollars if you are a minority. So you are worth more as a minority." The conclusion he drew from this: "If you were offended back in 1790 about slavery"—and all of you who were offended in 1790, you know who you are— "do not answer the race question . . . Today they are asking the race question to try to increase slavery."

★ ★ ★

In his early days on Fox, Beck's racial worries were mostly about Hispanics. "You're called a racist for just wanting a fence," he protested one night. But on his radio show, he found sinister connotations in the president's name. "You don't take the name Barack to identify with America," he said. "You take the name Barack to identify with what? Your heritage? The heritage, maybe, of your father in Kenya, who is a radical?"

Apparently the neonatal Obama should have raised an objection back in 1961.

Gradually, Beck's race monologues took a darker turn. In May 2009, he hosted the spokesman for ACORN. After a testy exchange, he returned from a commercial break to announce that he had kicked the ACORN man off the set.

"I thought he said I hate black people," Beck reported to his viewers.

Actually, a colleague informed Beck, the spokesman said Beck was "afraid" of black people.

Beck then turned to his next guest, the *Wall Street Journal*'s John Fund: "Are you afraid of black people or do you just hate them, John?"

Then, just before the White House "beer summit" that would cause Beck so much grief, he found a reason for his fear of black people—in particular, one black man named Obama.

"Here's the one thing tonight," he declared. "Everything that is getting pushed through Congress, including this health-care bill, [is] transforming America. And they are all driven by President Obama's thinking on one idea: Reparations."

Huh?

Actually, Obama opposed reparations to African Americans—but that, Beck decided, was only because "he doesn't think reparations would go far enough." He then began to spar with the straw man: "Three hundred sixty thousand in the Civil War, that wasn't enough?"

Beck had finally cracked Obama's secret code. "These massive programs are Obama-brand reparations. Obama is no dummy," he concluded. "His goal is creating a new America. A new model. A model that will settle old racial scores through new social justice."

The beer summit loomed, and Beck upped the rhetorical volume as he talked about "radical black nationalism" in the White House and "Marxist black liberation theology" influencing Obama. "We have demonstrated President Obama's desire for racial justice, but how is he setting out to achieve it? . . . Through intimidation, vilification, bullying, a system, an underground shell game."

The next morning, Beck went on *Fox & Friends* and called Obama a racist with deep-seated hatred for white people, or perhaps white culture.

Liberal activists launched a campaign to persuade Beck's advertisers to drop the show—and, over time, scores did. Beck went on the radio to denounce "the latest rage in the Glenn Beck tear-him-apart business."

His "deep-seated hatred" allegation? "I stand by that. I deem him a racist based on really his own standard of racism."

But as the criticism continued, even from conservatives, Beck began to see himself as a persecuted minority. "It is time to stand up and speak without fear," he coached his listeners. To help them, he brought in a psychiatrist, Fox News contributor Keith Ablow, and put himself on the couch.

"This is what people have said about me just this week," Beck told the doctor. "I'm a freak show, a religious nut job, hysterical, a cult leader, a shameless opportunist, a political operative . . . I'm full of crap—that one. Delusional, hard right, idiotic, thickheaded, spineless coward—I love that. Crybaby—that one they probably have me on. And I'm just a fear-mongering whatever."

Dr. Ablow soothed his patient: "People are so intoxicated right now. They have been told so many stories that if you're going to say the emperor has no clothes and stop the party, you're going to be vilified."

Beck's therapy session revived his righteousness: "The worst thing in my life is to lose my honor and to return—I am a religious nut job . . . to return to my heavenly father without honor, without doing what I was supposed to do."

Renewed by on-air psychotherapy, Beck turned his guns on the aforementioned Van Jones. "The president has tried to pass himself off as a guy who just sat in Jeremiah Wright's, you know, black liberation theology church for twenty years," the host said. "What is it this time? What is the excuse now for appointing the same kind of radical to an influential position in our government? Are white people poisoning people of color? Yes or no, Mr. President?"

The next night, Beck resumed the attack on Jones: "He's a black nationalist. He wants to spread the wealth around. He says that whites are poisoning minorities and immigrants [are] being sprayed by toxins by Americans. Good God Almighty, is it not unreasonable to ask for answers on this?"

Jones resigned soon after, but other battles in the race wars were just beginning; it was time for Beck to defend Joe Wilson against claims from black members of Congress that his shouting of "You lie" at the president during a speech to Congress had racial overtones.

"Do you want to call somebody a racist?" Beck dared. "If you do, you better have some facts to back it up." He quickly reconsidered this point. "But in today's America, does anybody even care?"

Not if the 5 P.M. ratings on Fox News are any indication.

Beck was growing increasingly bold. "I don't think people buy into the cries of racism," he proposed one night in September 2009.

"People are sick and tired of it," agreed his guest, conservative writer David Horowitz.

To test this theory, Horowitz tried some incendiary lines: "Blacks are the human shield of the Democratic

Party . . . that makes the Democratic Party a party of racists . . . The Democratic Party is the party of slavery, of segregation, of race preferences.

"Just get rid of the white guilt," Horowitz counseled. "Just forget it. Blacks all over the world want to come to America because it's the best place in the world for black people."

Appearing on the *CBS Evening News*, Beck was asked by Katie Couric if he was sorry he called Obama a racist. He was not about to make a recantation. "It is a serious question that I think needs serious discussion," he said. Beck would only allow that "I'm sorry the way it was phrased."

"Living in a sound-bite world is really a nasty place to live," he concluded.

You might even say it enslaves him.

CHAPTER 16
THE 9/12 MOVEMENT

Let us proclaim the mystery of faith.

Why do people follow Glenn Beck with such passion and devotion? This is a mystery only if you think of him in terms of his job description: conservative commentator. His followers do not view him primarily as a TV host or a talk-radio host. They regard him as more of a heavenly host.

Beck made his transformation from commentator to leader of a religious movement shortly after his arrival at Fox News. "On Friday," he told his followers one night in March 2009, "I'm going to show you the way to really save our country. But it's not—I'm not leading a movement or anything. It is you and people all over the country who believe in the nine principles and twelve values."

Not leading a movement or anything? Beck had contradicted himself before he drew his next breath. The "nine principles and twelve values" are a quasi-religious doctrine Beck authored after polling his flock. They were part of an advocacy movement he called the "9/12 Project."

The deliberate use of numbers for these "principles" and "values" echoed great attestations of faith that had come before: Martin Luther's ninety-five theses, Maimonides' thirteen principles of faith, and, perhaps most relevant, Joseph Smith's thirteen articles of faith for the Mormon Church. Beck portrayed himself as a modern-day Moses as he discussed his principles. A guest on his show one evening observed that Beck's precepts were quite reasonable because "you only have to follow seven of the nine—that was your original mandate."

"I know," Beck said. "It's like who can't agree with the Ten Commandments? Okay, 'well I don't like that one, I really want to make graven images.' Okay, give me seven out of ten."

Beck's principles ranged from the overtly religious ("I believe in God and He is the Center of my Life") to the secular, angry, and ungrammatical ("I work hard for what I have and I will share it with who I want to. Government cannot force me to be charitable"). His values are a standard mix of hope, reverence, courage, and the like.

The 9/12 Project, however, was more than a covenant with his followers. He used it as a basis for a mass revival meeting for the Church of Beck on the National Mall in

Washington. It was, appropriately enough, scheduled for September 12, 2009—hence 9/12—and was meant to evoke the feelings of patriotism and unity Americans experienced after the 2001 terrorist attacks. That's the thinking behind Beck principle #1: "America is good."

After this event, Beck immediately set to work on his next mass rally. He would assemble his flock at the Lincoln Memorial on August 28, 2010, the anniversary of the day in 1963 when the Reverend Martin Luther King Jr. stood on that very spot and delivered his "I Have a Dream" speech. This was timed, by pure serendipity, no doubt, with the expected release of a new Beck book, *The Plan*, about his hundred-year blueprint for America.

The man who called the first black president a racist was attempting to claim the mantle of the martyred Dr. King? This took chutzpah. But whatever qualities Beck lacks, chutzpah is not among them.

"It is the anniversary of the 'I Have a Dream' speech from Martin Luther King, and what an appropriate day!" Beck told his listeners. "I think it was almost divine providence, I do. His dream has been so corrupted. It's time we pick the dream back up and we finish the job."

Beck, unveiling his plans for his MLK moment, told a large crowd at a retirement community in Florida in November 2009 (at a signing for another of his books, *Arguing with Idiots*) that he would develop "a hundred-year plan for America." With this good doctrine, he preached to his disciples, "You will change the course of history." Casting aside one of his twelve values, "humility," Beck later forecast that his rally would be "one for the history books" and "a turning point in America."

The local paper reported that people camped out in line overnight for one of the wristbands that would allow them to have their copies of Beck's book autographed by the author. Speculation in advance of Beck's big speech was that he would announce a bid for public office, and journalists spotted a "Glenn Beck for President" sign in the crowd. But such rumors misunderstood what Beck was about: He didn't want the accountability of being an officeholder, he wanted the power of a movement leader.

Beck, his shirttails untucked from his jeans and his sleeves rolled up, promised nothing less than to "take our country back and usher in the next generation of Americans." To do this, he would hold a series of conventions around the country and assemble a "team of advisers" to give him policy prescriptions.

This man was no mere talk-show host.

As in his political philosophy, Beck was preceded in his advocacy movement by the controversial Mormon thinker Cleon Skousen, who once went around the country giving "Making of America" seminars on the Constitution. And Beck himself had dabbled in mass-movement politics back in 2003, when he created the "Rallies for America" in response to antiwar protests. Then a syndicated radio host, Beck timed the rallies, in cities from Sacramento to Philadelphia, with the release of yet another of his books, *The Real America*—establishing the pattern of rallies pegged to book releases that he would use repeatedly. This raises some doubts about Beck's adherence to "sincerity" on his list of values.

The events were full of patriotic imagery and patriotic bands playing patriotic songs. The experience, generally arranged by local radio stations that carried Beck, sometimes included church services. Beck would pull up in a painted "Rally for America" bus also labeled "The Glenn Beck Show" and wave from an observation deck atop the bus. The final event, in West Virginia, included a flyover and a recorded message from President George W. Bush. It was broadcast on Armed Forces Radio and included an appearance by the family of Jessica Lynch, the rescued prisoner of war in Iraq whose capture had been spun by the U.S. military into a false account of her firing at Iraqis.

After coming to Fox, Beck traveled freely back and forth between the worlds of commentary and political advocacy. He offered his audience "a specific plan of action" for taking control of America. On the radio, he asked Congresswoman Michele Bachmann, an outspoken Minnesota conservative, "How can I help you raise money? We should have a fund-raiser for you." He counseled listeners that "the best way to get the Republicans to change is to abandon them—leave." He determined that the Republican candidate in a special congressional election in upstate New York was "not a Republican" and urged support for her conservative challenger.

His first big advocacy campaign at Fox came with the "FNC Tax Day Tea Parties" on April 15, 2009. Barack Obama had been in office for two and a half months. "Americans across the country are holding tea parties to let politicians know that we have had enough," he announced on air. "Celebrate with Fox News." He told his radio listeners to join him at his own tax-day Tea Party, at the Alamo in San Antonio, with Ted Nugent. "The costs are going crazy," he added, so "I'm going to do a fund-raiser" for the Tea Party group hosting him. "I've heard it's like $500 a plate or something like that." Never mind those Beck values of "thrift" and "moderation."

Five days before the big event, Beck had an actor, Bob Basso, dress up in Colonial garb and pretend to be Thomas Paine reading Beck's summons to action:

> The time for talk is over. Enough is enough. Your democracy has deteriorated to government of the government, by the government, and for the government. On April 15th, that despicable arrogance will be soundly challenged for the whole world to see. Our friends will applaud it. Our enemies will fear it, an unprecedented moment of citizen response not

seen in recent history since December 7th, 1941. Millions of your fellow Americans, neighbors, friends, relatives will bring their anger and their determination into the streets . . . Join the April 15th tea parties and the 9/12 Project elevating us above petty policies and uniting us with a national discussion of values and principles as our Founding Fathers originally envisioned.

This modern-day Paine, at Beck's direction, likened the Obama administration's stimulus plan to the terrorist attacks of 2001:

Your complacency will only aid and abet to our national suicide. Remember, they wouldn't dare bomb Pearl Harbor, but they did. They wouldn't dare drive two planes into the World Trade Center, but they did. They wouldn't dare pilot a plane through the most sophisticated air defenses in the world and crash into the Pentagon, but they did. They wouldn't dare pass the largest spending bill in history in open defiance of the will of the people, but they did . . . The power to change the course of history comes to very few people in a lifetime. On April 15th, you can take the first step. The second step is a one-million 'we the people' march on Washington.

When the dead patriot was done, Beck offered his conclusion: "See you at the Alamo."

To spur participation, Beck tossed in a bit of paranoid talk in his radio show on April 13. "I'm going to be a little cryptic here," he began, and indeed he was. "There are forces at play that are doing everything they can to make this tax day at San Antonio at the Alamo about me." This was unsurprising, because Beck himself had organized and promoted the event, with liberal use of the first-person pronoun. "They're trying to—we have some very good reports; we have a very good security team—the final straw was there are just things that . . . everything is out of control right now because people will do whatever they have to, to destroy the message."

Beck didn't quite explain himself, but he did back out as the keynote speaker of the event. This, however, was a distinction without a difference, because he was the de facto center of the event anyway, as he did his live broadcast from the Alamo. "Tens of thousands if not hundreds of thousands are gathered on street corners, state capitols, or in front of their town squares all across our country today for Tax Day tea parties," a triumphant Beck proclaimed from the Alamo on tax day. He riled the crowd to boo the media and switched between music and stories of the Alamo in 1836—where the surrounded and outnumbered Americans fought the Mexicans, though they knew they would die.

"This is why I think there is no better place for a tea party because this is the—this is kind of the attitude that I'm sensing from people all over the country," Beck said. The Tea Party activists were preparing for a heroic and bloody last stand? "I believe, and all over the country sense that we've got to draw a line in the sand and say—no more!" he declared. "I have a feeling something big is starting with the tea parties."

Beck was determined to get out in front of this parade. He channeled the Tea Party anger into his own march on Washington, which came five months later. He had already telegraphed the beginning of the 9/12 Project months earlier, in January 2009, when he stated that the nation's problems could be solved "by just being the people that we promised ourselves we would be on 9/12, the day after 9/11."

Beck was probably right about that; the days following the attacks were a time of great national unity and purpose. He even made noises about making his movement an apolitical denunciation of Republicans as well as Democrats. But it quickly became a movement of aggrieved conservatives. The tax-day protests had attracted a fiercely anti-Obama crowd, and some carried signs with racist imagery or demands that Obama produce his birth certificate to prove that he's American.

Beck, to his credit, didn't embrace the "birther" theory,

but he found a way of validating his followers' grievances, whatever they were. He gave voice to them with a "You Are Not Alone" special on Fox to promote his 9/12 Project. Beck followers, using Meetup.com, held watch parties throughout the land; total viewership topped three million.

"Every time you turn that television on, it just seems like the whole world is spinning out of control," he told his viewers in an open monologue interrupted by frequent breaks for crying. "What happened to the country that loved the underdog and stood up for the little guy? What happened to the voice of the 'forgotten man'? The 'forgotten' man is you. But something is happening in America. The paradigm is about to change." Beck's answer: "Let's find ourselves and our solutions together, again, with the nine founding principles and the twelve eternal values."

After a good cry ("I'm sorry. I just love my country. And I fear for it"), Beck pivoted to paranoia. "It seems like the voices of our leaders and special interest and the media, they're surrounding us. It sounds intimidating, but you know what? Pull away the curtain and you'll realize that there isn't anybody there. It's just a few people that are just pressing the buttons and their voices are actually really weak. The truth is—they don't surround us. We surround them."

To illustrate, he introduced a mosaic he had constructed out of photos sent in by his viewers. They were arranged to form a hand clasping a flagpole with an American flag. The words "We the People" and "9/12 Project" were at the bottom. Beck directed his followers to report for duty on September 12.

Bill O'Reilly asked Beck after the show if this might be called a "revival meeting."

"It's a grassroots movement," Beck explained.

So it turns out he did see himself as a movement leader, after all.

Beck drummed up support for the movement almost nightly on air. "The site was shut down for almost thirty hours because it was getting hit by 500 people 500 times a second . . . We already have 250,000 people that have joined the '912Project.com' . . . Now, there are more than 400,000 members." He recommended to followers the slogan "We surround them. We're not alone. That is the mantra." He adopted as his own Benjamin Franklin's "Join or Die" cartoon showing a snake divided (instead of the original eight pieces, Beck's had ten: nine for the nine principles and one piece, the tail, for the twelve values).

"Now is the time to stand up and make your voice heard. Come on—follow me!" Beck said at the start of another 9/12 Project special in May. "Declare yourself a 9/12-er, and come on—follow me!" he said at the start of a show days later. He kept his TV and radio audiences up-to-date about his planned rally in Washington on September 12.

"I gave you the 9/12 Project," Beck told his followers in August, once again playing Moses. He said he "prayed about" whether to speak at the Washington rally, but decided he would be more useful anchoring coverage of the event from the comfort of the TV studio. "I laid out a plan called the 9/12 Project," he reminded his audience one night. As an additional incentive to participate, he likened Congress to terrorists and Nazis with a musical video promoting the event. It said: "In the beginning, King George underestimated. Many have underestimated. Hitler underestimated. The world underestimated. Terrorists underestimated the will of the American people! Congress, please don't underestimate the will of the American people." Next to a photo of a grinning Beck, the final frame said: "Saturday 9/12, 1–3 P.M. E.T. Fox News Channel. It's Time to Stand Up."

Beck radiated a certain pride of ownership as he anchored Fox's coverage of the event on the big day. His rallying cry had brought in many of the usual suspects from past demonstrations: those carrying aborted fetus pictures and posters of Obama in whiteface as the Joker from Batman, now coupled with a suggestion to "Bury Obamacare with Kennedy" that played on Ted Kennedy's death a couple of weeks earlier. There were also plenty of "Thank you, Glenn Beck" and "Glenn Beck for President" signs. From the comfort of his studio, Beck reported with confidence that "this is a collection of people who have never probably marched before."

Beck brought in his correspondent at the rally. Fox News's Griff Jenkins ran along a fence and whipped up the crowd on the other side of it.

"You guys got a message for Glenn Beck?" he shouted. The crowd cheered. "Glenn, it's unbelievable," Jenkins continued. "Thousands and thousands of people. Look at this crowd right there." Turning his microphone to the crowd, he asked again, "You got something to say to Glenn Beck?" The crowd cheered again. "Glenn, it's one mile from the Capitol back to the monument, and that sea of people goes all the way! That's one mile of people!"

After generating a couple more cheers from the crowd, Jenkins informed the anchor that the crowd had "a lot of salutes" for Beck. "If this is an uprising, we are at the beginning of a political movement," he reported.

"Wow," Beck replied.

It was indeed a "wow" moment. Beck's nascent political movement had motivated tens of thousands of people to march on Washington. But even that impressive reality was not sufficient for Beck. On Monday, he was back behind his microphone, creating fiction. "The *London Telegraph* is now saying the numbers [were] over a million. They quote a source from the National Parks Service saying that is the largest march on Washington ever."

In fact, the *Telegraph* reported no such thing. "Tens of thousands of conservative 'tea party' protesters have staged the biggest demonstration of Barack Obama's presidency," the newspaper reported.

On the *Fox & Friends* morning show, Beck declared that "we had a university, I think it's University of—I don't remember what university it is, look at the pictures," he said, and "1.7 million that crowd was estimated at."

"Wow, because we were saying tens of thousands," the *Fox & Friends* host observed.

"University looked at it, did the body count," Beck assured her, never coming up with the name of "university." (Beck principle #3: "I must always try to be a more honest person than I was yesterday.")

Beck, flush with success, was dropping his earlier insistence that he was not a movement leader. "In many ways, you are sort of the cable news poster child for these tea parties," Fox's Greta Van Susteren asked him on air. "Fair description?"

"I guess it's fair to be able to say that, on the fact that, six months ago, I said that we need to reconnect with our values and our principles, and I laid out the 9/12 Project, the nine values and twelve principles, and that is part of what this has come out of," Beck answered. "Yes, so I think that's fair." (More than fair, in fact. Beck would later say that the Tea Party movement was doing "exactly what

I laid out" and that the Republican Party was emulating his nine principles.)

The rally over, Beck turned his 9/12 Project Web site into something of a bulletin board for the Tea Party movement. "4/21: Action Request from the Florida Tea Party . . . 5/24: 9/12ers Make A Difference in Colorado's Elections!" And a couple of months after the 9/12 rally, he was ready to announce his followers' next pilgrimage to Washington. "It's a multilevel plan," Beck told O'Reilly. "Now the next phase is coming."

The next phase would be Beck's following in Martin Luther King Jr.'s footsteps to the Lincoln Memorial, forty-seven years to the day later. He had a snazzy logo drawn up, showing Honest Abe in his chair and the words "Restoring Honor." Beck announced that the event would benefit the Special Operations Warrior Foundation, a non-profit that helps the families of wounded or fallen special ops forces. But the small print told a slightly different story: The charity would pay the cost of—and take the financial risk for—Beck's rally. "All contributions made to the Special Operations Warrior Foundation (SOWF) will first be applied to the costs of the Restoring Honor Rally," the small print said. "All contributions in excess of these costs will then be retained by the SOWF."

In preparation for the big event, Beck announced, he would have "a series of conventions" to teach his followers how to organize. He referred to that "100-year plan" developed with "top experts." And he mentioned in an aside that the rally in Washington would be tied to the release of his new book, *The Plan*. It would, he said, be the "birthday of a new national movement to restore our great country."

The first part of Beck's hundred-year plan failed to materialize. Other than gatherings in Orlando and Salt Lake City, his promised conventions didn't happen. But something better happened. Beck lured a solid lineup of singers and entertainers to perform at the Lincoln Memorial, and he recruited the only person who rivals him in pull with the Tea Party movement—the former governor of Alaska.

"I think it's going to be the most inspiring—and for me, personally, the most humbling—experience, could be, of my lifetime," Sarah Palin informed Beck and his listeners on his radio show. "I hope we have a million people there to honor our troops. I'm just so absolutely thrilled that you invited me and I wouldn't miss it for the world."

Governor Palin needn't have worried about the crowd size; regardless of the actual numbers, Beck would find somebody—a foreign news outlet or a "university" somewhere—to say it was more than a million.

More interesting was Palin's claim that appearing at a Glenn Beck rally could be the most humbling experience of her life. Sarah Palin, humbled in the presence of Beck? That's not a movement leader—that's a messiah.

CHAPTER 17

GLENN BECK IS NOT RESPONSIBLE FOR ANY ACTS OF VIOLENCE COMMITTED BY HIS VIEWERS; HE'S JUST AN ENTERTAINER

* *

Early on a Saturday morning, April 4, 2009, Pittsburgh police were called to a domestic disturbance in the city's Stanton Heights neighborhood on the east side. The routine call would become the deadliest ever for the police department.

Awaiting the police at a ranch house was Richard Poplawski, a troubled twenty-two-year-old man wearing a bulletproof vest and armed with an AK-47, a .22 rifle, and a handgun. Within minutes, three cops were dead: Eric Kelly, the father of three daughters; Stephen Mayhle, the father of two daughters; and Paul Sciulo III, engaged to be married.

Sciulo and Mayhle were both fatally shot in the head when the door opened. Kelly, who was on his way home from his shift and stopped by to help, was shot and killed when he got out of his car.

Poplawski surrendered after a standoff with a SWAT team that lasted nearly four hours. Hundreds of shots were fired.

Soon after this, the Anti-Defamation League reported that the killer had, in the weeks before the shooting, posted a video clip of Beck talking on March 3 about the FEMA camps with Representative Ron Paul of Texas. "FEMA is already very, very powerful and they overrule when they go in on emergencies. So in some ways, they can accomplish what you might be thinking about setting up camps," Paul told Beck in the interview.

Poplawski had posted a link of the YouTube video to Stormfront, a neo-Nazi Web site. The shooter also posted on the Web site news that Pittsburgh was "ramping up the police state" when it put surveillance cameras on downtown bridges, and he said he had warned grocery customers to stock up on canned goods. These, the Anti-Defamation League said, were part of the conspiracy theories of "the New World Order, planned gun confiscations, and government plots against the citizenry." These were all Beck themes. Conspiracy theories from the 1990s were revived, including SHTF (shit hits the fan) and TEOTWAWKI (the end of the world as we know it)—strong Beck currents.

The shooting came after Beck told his millions of viewers that he "can't debunk" the notion that FEMA was operating a concentration camp in Wyoming—but before he finally admitted, cagily, that the conspiracy theory wasn't true.

Is Beck to be blamed for those five girls in Pittsburgh losing their dads? That goes a bit too far; it's impossible to know what went through the mind of a mentally unstable killer. But the episode does show how Beck's words are inspiring the fringe, and bringing some of their wacky theories into the mainstream.

Beck has periodically warned his viewers against violence. "Let me be clear on one thing: If someone tries to harm another person in the name of the Constitution or the truth behind 9/11 or anything else, they are just as dangerous and crazy as those people we don't seem to recognize anymore, you know, the ones who kill in the name of Allah," he said on his TV show just days before the Pittsburgh killing.

Yet at the same time, his shows are full of violent thoughts and offerings:

"The clock is ticking," he said one night. "I fear for the future. Somebody is going to do something stupid and it will change the republic overnight," he added, snapping his fingers. He then went on to discuss President Obama's "death panels."

"America, you're being set up," he said after the health-care legislation passed. "And it is only a matter of time before an actual crazy person really does something stupid."

Beck had a guest on his show, outspoken former CIA official Michael Scheuer, to say: "The only chance we have as a country right now is for Osama bin Laden to deploy and detonate a major weapon in the United States . . . Only Osama can execute an attack which will force Americans to demand that their government protect them effectively, consistently, and with as much violence as necessary."

Beck joined in: "Which is why, I was thinking this weekend, if I were him, that would be the last thing I would do right now."

Beck has proposed poisoning Nancy Pelosi, hitting Charlie Rangel over the head with a shovel, and shooting Michael Moore—all in good fun, of course. He says on air that people in the Obama administration are trying to kill him. And he uses terms of war to describe his fight with the political opposition:

"A lot of people in America are probably feeling a little defeated," he told Fox viewers as the health-care legislation neared final passage. "But I want you to know: Do not feel that way. The battle was lost, the war is not over. The war is just beginning."

A few days later, he sent out a message on Twitter in ransom-note style: "Attn: 60's sanfran radicals—we will rise and crush in Nov. Together like NEVER b4. You WILL fail bcause We R COMING. C it @5 on FNC."

While Beck disavows violence, he also encourages viewers to read between the lines and infer things that he does not say aloud. Speaking on his radio show in July 2009 of an Obama administration "thugocracy," he warned:

"Please don't let this message fall on deaf ears. Please. I fear that there will come a time when I cannot say things that I am currently saying. I fear that it will come to television and to radio, and I will stop saying these things. Understand me clearly. Hear me now: If I ever stop saying these things, you will know why. Because I will have made a choice that I can only say certain things, and I haven't lost all of the rights. But know that these things are true. And if you hear me stop saying these things, it's because I can no longer say them to you. But hear them between the sentences. Hear them, please. I will be screaming them to you."

For those inclined to hear voices, that screaming can be heard quite loudly.

In April 2010, a man by the name of Greg Giusti with a history of mental problems was arrested for threatening Pelosi, the woman Beck had pretended to poison on his set. Giusti had made dozens of calls to Pelosi and, reciting her home address, warned that she should not support health-care legislation if she wanted to see her home again.

In Pelosi's hometown of San Francisco, KGO-TV reached Giusti's eighty-three-year-old mother, Eleanor.

"Greg has—frequently gets in with a group of people that have really radical ideas and that are not consistent with myself or the rest of the family and—which gets him into problems," she told the station. "And apparently I would say this must be another one that somehow he's gotten onto either by—I'd say Fox News or all of those that are really radical, and he—that's where he comes from."

Fox News: And it's a safe bet she wasn't talking about *Special Report with Bret Baier*, or *Your World with Neil Cavuto*.

A crazy person watching Beck could have thought he was doing the world a favor by taking on this violent Nancy Pelosi. Beck listed Pelosi as one of the "really dangerous people" in California, including communists, socialists, and ecoterrorists. He accused her of "inciting" conservative demonstrators and "slapping them across the face."

A couple of weeks before Giusti's arrest, Beck beckoned to photos of people including Obama and Pelosi and called them "dangerous." He asked: "You'd pick up a gun? Have you ever thought of that? These people have. Because possibly, maybe the question should be asked, maybe they're tired of evolution, and maybe they are waiting for revolution."

On the same show, Beck ventured: "I'd never thought about revolution. I've never thought about armed insurrection or bombing or anything like that. Then I looked at the other side of the board and I realized—wow, the people around the president have. Not only have they thought about it, many of them have plotted it. Some of them were actually engaged in bomb throwing."

The previous night, Beck had delivered his plea to "those of you in the administration who are coming after me" to remember the commandment "Thou shall not kill."

During this same period of post-health-reform attacks, Beck said that Obama had "just punched you in the face with health care" and asserted that "most of the country feel like they've been spanked over health care."

So if the Democrats are trying to hurt or kill Beck and his followers, can the Democrats be hurt or killed in self-defense? Disturbed minds would have to wonder. "You can try to put the lid on this group of people, but you will never silence us," Beck said on his radio show. "You will never—you can shoot me in the head, you can shoot the next guy in the head, but there will be ten others that line up."

In June 2010, Beck returned to his "shoot me" dare. "Shoot me in the head before I stop talking about the Founders. Shoot me in the head if you try to change our government." And Beck evidently doesn't think such an act is far-fetched. "You have to be prepared to take rocks to the head," he advised his radio audience in May 2010. "The other side is attacking."

Violent talk is not new to Beck, but people probably didn't take it very seriously in the early years. "I've been coming up with a list of people that I want to kill with a shovel," he proposed on the radio in 2001, specifically suggesting that "we start" with Rangel, the New York Democratic congressman.

"I'm thinking about killing Michael Moore, and I'm wondering if I could kill him myself, or if I would need to hire somebody to do it," he said in 2005, the same year he admitted to "hating the 9/11 victims' families" because of their complaints. "No, I think I could" kill Moore, he continued. "I think he could be looking me in the eye, you know, and I could just be choking the life out—is this wrong?"

As in other areas, Beck's move to Fox brought the violent talk to a new level. As the town-hall meetings over health care heated up in the summer of 2009, he helped calm the situation by declaring that a coup was taking the country into dictatorship: "There is a coup going on. There is a stealing of America. And the way it is done, it is being done through the guise of an election but they lie to us the entire time . . . And they're going to say they did it democratically and they're going to grab power every way they can, and God help us in an emergency."

The imagery grew more and more colorful: Beck, as previously mentioned, pretending to pour gasoline on a guest and asking, "President Obama, why don't you just set us on fire?"; Beck proposing to "run those who are bankrupting our country and literally stealing our children's future out of town. Grab a torch!"; Beck calling his opponents "bloodsucker vampires" and concluding that "either the economy becomes like a walking dead or you drive a stake through the heart of the bloodsuckers."

More than once, he has invoked secession as a solution to conservatives' objections—suggesting the fanciful notion of a civil war over health-care reform. "Texas is going to be surrounded. You need a giant moat of fire," he said one day. "Wouldn't that be great?"

Civil war? Great! Tell us more.

"If push comes to shove," he continued; "if nullification [of health care and other laws] does not stand, if I can't nullify the things that you're doing to us, then we secede because Texans are serious about secession." Beck likes this idea so much that he has spoken of moving from his Connecticut mansion to Texas. "You're going to have the feds coming, you're going to have a flood going from America into Texas."

Another time, Beck told listeners that "you can't convince me that the Founding Fathers wouldn't allow you to secede. The Constitution is not a suicide pact and if a state says I don't want to go there because that's suicide, they have a right to back out. People have a right not to commit economic suicide . . . I sign into this union and I can never ever get out? No matter what the government does, I can never get out? That only leaves you with one other option. That doesn't seem like a good option."

Except for the moat of fire.

There are less provocative ways for Beck to make his point, but that wouldn't bring in three million viewers a night and eight million radio listeners a week. He doesn't merely voice disagreement with progressives, he says, "I'm going to be like the Israeli Nazi hunters . . . To the day I die I am going to be a progressive hunter. I am going to find the people who did this to our country and expose them, I don't care if they're in nursing homes."

Beck doesn't merely voice his displeasure with health-care reform. He says: "We need to fight hard within the rules and pray, get down on your knees and pray, pray. It is September 11th all over again except we didn't have the collapsing buildings, but we need God more than ever."

He doesn't raise objections to Democrats' legislative tactics. He makes a gun with his hand and says: "They are putting a gun to America's head. Pass this or we all die! Yes, they're doing that."

He doesn't state his differences with Obama's advisers Cass Sunstein and John Holdren. He says: "Between health-care and the environment those two men, in the wrong conditions, will be responsible for many, many deaths."

He doesn't raise worries about where liberal policies are taking the country. He says: "They are taking you to a place to be slaughtered."

Hunters. Slaughter. Death. Die. Gun to the head. What are people to do with these violent images? Beck has an idea: Ambush lawmakers with them—at their homes.

When a caller to Beck's radio show in August 2009 expressed his frustration that his congressman wasn't attending his Tea Party gathering, Beck suggested: "Hold a meeting in front of their house if you have to . . . Hold these people responsible. If you know they go shopping on Saturday at Safeway, get in the parking lot at Safeway." Another time, he told his followers to come to Washington and "look 'em in the whites of their eyes." If that wasn't clear, he added: Things are "coming to a point where the people will have exhausted all their options. When that happens, look out. Look out."

Beck gives his audience every reason to be desperate. "We are a country that is headed towards socialism, totalitarianism, beyond your wildest imagination," he warns them. And: "Anti-God forces are aligning themselves all over the world and here at home." And: "These guys have to worry about the bullets put into their backs by our politicians."

It sounds like a call to fight back by any means necessary—but of course Beck is often cautioning his followers to follow Gandhi's admonition to use "truth as your anvil" and warning them that "just one lunatic like Timothy McVeigh could ruin everything."

But how does somebody become Timothy McVeigh?

Beck himself offered an interesting view on this, in a conversation with Fox's Bill O'Reilly. The two were discussing a gunman who killed ten people and himself in an Alabama shooting spree. "Here is a guy who felt that he had been wronged . . . He was disgruntled and everything else, and then he went out and shot a bunch of people," Beck explained. "But as I'm listening to him, I'm thinking about the American people that feel disenfranchised right now, that feel like nobody's hearing their voice. The government isn't hearing their voice . . . If you're a conservative, you are called a racist, you want to starve children, yada, yada, yada. They're—and every time they do speak out, they are shut down by political correctness. How do you not have those people turn into that guy?"

Beck had just suggested that the government, with political correctness, was turning Americans into mass murderers.

"Well, look," O'Reilly intervened. "Nobody, even if they're frustrated, is going to hurt another human being unless they're mentally ill, I think."

Beck thought otherwise. "If they're pushed to the wall, you don't think people get pushed to the wall?"

"No, I don't believe in the snap thing," O'Reilly said. "I think that kind of violence is inside you and it's a personality disorder."

It's a fascinating question: Will otherwise normal

people "snap" if they are made to feel pushed to the wall? Beck, at 5 P.M. each weekday, seems determined to test the hypothesis.

In July 2010, an unemployed carpenter named Byron Williams, pulled over for erratic driving in Oakland, California, got in a shootout with police with his 9mm handgun, shotgun, and .309-caliber rifle with armor-piercing bullets. Captured after injuring two officers, the parolee told investigators that he wanted "to start a revolution" by "killing people of importance at the Tides Foundation and the ACLU." His mother, Janice, told the *San Francisco Chronicle* that her son had been watching television news and was upset by "the way Congress was railroading through all these left-wing agenda items."

And what television news show could have directed the troubled man's ire toward the obscure Tides Foundation? There was only one. "Tides was one of the hardest things that we ever tried to explain, and everyone told us that we couldn't," Beck boasted to his radio listeners a week after the shooting. "The reason why the blackboard really became what the blackboard is, is because I was trying to explain Tides and how all of this worked." He savored the fact that "no one knew what Tides was until the blackboard." For good measure, Beck went after Tides again on Fox the next four nights.

ACKNOWLEDGMENTS

* *

This book would not have been completed on schedule—
and quite possibly not at all—without the heroic efforts of
Emily Kotecki. Glenn Beck has a whole squad of research-
ers, but all of them combined don't have the talent of Emily,
my former colleague at the *Washington Post,* who spent
hours combing the Web and transcribing Beck oddities and
ironies. Her work and mine were made easier by the hundreds of hours of recordings of Beck's TV and radio shows
posted online by the many organizations Beck most loves to
hate, particularly Media Matters for America.

I am profoundly grateful to Bill Thomas, editor in chief
at Doubleday, who, owing to some inexplicable lapse in
his otherwise excellent judgment, continues to publish my
work. He saw the potential for this book in a 750-word
column I wrote, strengthened me when I wavered, and,

together with his able assistant Coralie Hunter, magically threaded my musings into a cohesive and at times coherent narrative. My agent, the inimitable Rafe Sagalyn, is the one who married my inchoate wish to write about the coarsening political discourse with a focus on the phenomenon that is Beck.

My research benefited from the suggestions of many journalistic colleagues, particularly a brave few at Fox News who gave me a sense of Beck from the inside (and who, for reasons of job preservation, will not be named here). This book should not be seen as a screed against Fox; I have worked with many first-rate correspondents and producers at the network, and they more than anybody have suffered because of Beck. I have appeared on Fox in the past as a commentator and would gladly do so again in the unlikely event I get the call.

I appreciate the willingness of Marcus Brauchli, Liz Spayd, and the other editors on the news side of the *Washington Post* to let me undertake this project. I am indebted to Fred Hiatt and his staff on the editorial side of the *Post* for inviting me to write a regular op-ed column. This new form has expanded my thinking and allowed me to explore a broader range of topics—leading to a column titled "The Beck Effect" in January 2010 that was the genesis of this book.

I extend my thanks to friends and family who toler-

ACKNOWLEDGMENTS

ated (or, perhaps, enjoyed) my disappearance from civilization these last several months. Above all, I thank the two most important people in my life, my wife, Donna, and my daughter, Paola, for their patience, support, and love during the many nights and weekends I spent producing this book. They are my sustenance on good days and bad days—and, should Beck turn out to be correct, there is nobody I'd rather be with on doomsday.

ABOUT THE AUTHOR

Dana Milbank is a syndicated columnist with the *Washington Post* and, formerly, a prizewinning White House reporter. He is the author of three books, including the national bestseller *Homo Politicus*. He has also provided commentary for CNN, MSNBC, CNBC, and NPR. He received a B.A. in political science cum laude from Yale in 1990. He lives in Washington with his wife and daughter.